Management Information SYSTEMS

DANTES/DSST* Test Study Guide

All rights reserved. This Study Guide, Book and Flashcards are protected under the US Copyright Law. No part of this book or study guide or flashcards may be reproduced, distributed or stored in a retrieval system, or transmitted in any form or by any means, electronic, mechanical, photocopying, recording, or otherwise, without the prior written permission of the publisher Breely Crush Publishing, LLC.

© 2026 Breely Crush Publishing, LLC

DSST is a registered trademark of The Thomson Corporation and its affiliated companies, and does not endorse this book.

971032826143

Copyright ©2003 - 2026, Breely Crush Publishing, LLC.

All rights reserved.

This Study Guide, Book and Flashcards are protected under the US Copyright Law. No part of this publication may be reproduced, distributed or stored in a retrieval system, or transmitted in any form or by any means, electronic, mechanical, photocopying, recording, or otherwise, without the prior written permission of the publisher Breely Crush Publishing, LLC.

Published by Breely Crush Publishing, LLC
10808 River Front Parkway
South Jordan, UT 84095
www.breelycrushpublishing.com

ISBN-13: 978-1-61433-678-5

Printed and bound in the United States of America.

DSST is a registered trademark of The Thomson Corporation and its affiliated companies, and does not endorse this book.

Table of Contents

Foundations *1*
   Basic Terminology *1*
   Computer Literacy and Information Systems Literacy *2*
   Functions of MIS *3*
   Components of MIS *4*
   Attributes of Information as a Resource *5*
Systems Theory *6*
   Characteristics *6*
   Relevance to Information Systems *9*
Hardware and Software *11*
   History and Evolution of Hardware and Software *11*
   Information System Hardware *12*
   Information System Software *16*
   Information Architecture Terminology *20*
System Level *22*
   Individual Information Systems *22*
   Workgroup Information Systems *26*
   Organizational Information Systems *28*
   Interorganizational Information Systems *31*
Database Management *32*
   Data Models *32*
   Hierarchy of Data *35*
   Organizing Data *36*
   Data Query *36*
   Data Update *37*
   DBMS *38*
Analysis and Design of Systems *39*
   Traditional Systems Development Life Cycle (SDLC) *39*
   Contemporary Approaches *47*
   End-User Computing *49*
   Organization of MIS *50*
   Relationship of MIS to the Enterprise *51*
   Value of the MIS Function *53*
   MIS Administration and Management *54*
Telecommunications *55*
   Terminology *55*
   Networks *56*
   Relevance to Business *59*

Informational Support *64*
   Dimensions of Management Support *64*
   System Types *65*
Programming Languages *70*
   Traditional Programming Languages *70*
   Object-Oriented Programming Languages *70*
   Programming Languages for the Internet *71*
   Examples Code from Common Programming Languages *71*
Issues *74*
   Ethics *74*
   Security *77*
E-Commerce *78*
   Sample Test Questions *79*
   Test-Taking Strategies *119*
   Test Preparation *119*
   Legal Note *120*

FOUNDATIONS

Basic Terminology

Basic Terminology

The term **information systems (IS)** refers to all the processes, people, equipment, policies, and data that are needed to get information to where it is needed within an organization. The computers, fax machines, telephone systems, and other equipment used to make the transfer of information easier are called information technology.

Many information systems include a computer, but there are still some common manual systems. For example, some companies may use a filing cabinet to store their records instead of digitizing them. An information system that includes a computer is technically called a **computer information system (CIS)**.

Management information systems (MIS) organize information in ways useful to those making management decisions. Organizations may use MIS in many ways, including pinpointing targets for a new marketing campaign, determining the prices for a product line or deciding on a retail site. MIS are often used for "what if" scenarios. "What if" scenarios are predictions based on possible changes. Some examples of "what if" scenarios include:

- What would happen to our profits if we increased our prices by 5%?
- What would happen to our cash flow if we took out a loan?
- What would happen to our costs if we transferred some third shift workers to second shift?

Other terms for MIS are information reporting system and management reporting system. Transaction processing systems (TPSs), which include fail-safes and tests to help ensure that all of an organization's transactions are completed without error, are an important part of many management information systems.

 Computer Literacy and Information Systems Literacy

Computer Terminology

Because many information systems are computer-based, it is important to be familiar with technology terms.

The unit of data used by a computer is the bit (b). A bit is a binary digit, either zero or one. Eight bits are grouped together in a byte (B). A kilobyte (K or KB) is 1024 bytes and a megabyte (M or MB) is 1024 kilobytes. A gigabyte (G or GB), or "gig," equals 1024 megabytes. Data transfer rates are often given in kilobytes per second (KB/s) or megabytes per second (MB/s).

Access time, often given in milliseconds (ms), is the length of time between a request for information and the output from the system. Access time is a particular concern to IS professionals who design or maintain databases.

Random-access memory (RAM) is a measure of the amount of temporary memory a computer has for data processing. Read-only memory (ROM) is memory that can be read from, but not written to. Write once, read many (WORM) memory allows data to be saved to and read from, but not deleted or edited. WORM discs are often used to back up and store data.

Information Systems Terminology

A computer application is a single system within a computer that performs a related set of tasks.

EXAMPLES OF COMPUTER APPLICATIONS	
Application	*Function*
Word Processor	Facilitates creation, formatting and editing of written documents
Spreadsheet	Organizes tables of information and automates computations
Database	Organizes groups of data and allows user to sort them using combinations of attributes
Web browser	Allows the user to connect to, access and disconnect from the internet
Graphics editor	Facilitates the manipulation and conversion of graphics files

An information system can include many interconnected computer applications. A spreadsheet may call on information from a database, for example.

Information systems have four general functions:

- The **input function** allows new data to be entered into the system.
- The **storage function** holds the inputted data.
- The **processing function** allows users to manipulate stored data.
- The **output function** allows stored or manipulated data to be accessed.

The input function is usually achieved using hardware devices such as keyboards, touch screens, or scanners. The storage function usually relies on a database and may include a variety of media, including hard drives, CDs, tapes, or optical drives. The processing function may include complex statistical analysis and mathematical modeling. The resulting information may be outputted on a monitor or printer. The output function may occur on a regularly scheduled basis, at the user's demand, or both.

Functions of MIS

The four main functions of any information system are input, storage, processing, and output. MIS handles these functions in ways that may differ from other information systems.

The Input Function

An MIS usually uses internal data fed into the system by the transaction processing system (TPS). TPS is used in regulating and facilitating transactions. Electronic billing, payroll systems, and inventory management systems are all examples of TPS. The information collected by a TPS is like the basic operating information of a business. They can track sales data to be used by other information systems. TPSs capture, enter, and validate data. External data can be inputted into the MIS using several methods, including direct input into the MIS or download from an external database.

The Storage Function

Data in an MIS is usually stored in a database, although it may be stored in files. Databases are preferred because they often speed up data access.

The Processing Function

Processing in an MIS usually involves fairly simple mathematical computations. Sometimes the equations used are **recursive**. That is, they require input from previous iterations of the equation.

The Output Function

Management information systems produce output in the form of reports generated by user queries. A **query** is a request for specific information based on data in the system. There are several types of reports that an MIS can generate as output. A **detail report** lists the complete information generated by the data after the processing function. Some totals may also be included in a detail report. A **summary report** shows the totals for each group of data, but excludes the details. An **exception report** shows data that is excluded from specific criteria. For example, products that have not shown a specific profit over the course of the year might be included in an exception report.

Reports can also be classified according to how often they are generated. A **scheduled report** is prepared automatically at specific time intervals. **Demand reports** are only generated by the system upon user request. An **ad hoc report** is only prepared once.

Components of MIS

Management information systems can fulfill these functions by using information technology, human resources, and data.

- The **information technology** components of a management information system include hardware—the computers, fax machines, printers, input devices, and storage media in the system—and software. Software refers to the programs that control the hardware. Software can include applications, peripheral drivers, and operating systems.

- The **human resources** components of an information system include the people who run the system and the policies that the organization has in place for the access and use of the system. The personnel aspect of an information system includes everyone who inputs or accesses the data in the system, uses the hardware or software, or influences the IS policies. Information systems policies include documentation for how to use the hardware and software, and a code of ethics for using the system. An organization's code of ethics may discuss issues such as customer privacy, system security, access to the data, accuracy of the output, and ownership of the information.

- The **data** of the information system are the facts that the system inputs, stores, processes, and outputs. Data can be as simple as a single character. **Information** is data in a useful form. An information system may store a list of serial numbers. By itself, this list of serial numbers is probably not very useful. When correlated with other information in the system to provide a report of customers affected by a product recall, however, this data becomes useful information.

Levels of Management

Management information systems affect three levels of management. Operations management includes those decisions that affect the daily functioning of the organization. **Operations management** may deal with workforce scheduling, routinely ordering supplies, and fulfilling orders. **Middle management** includes intermediate-term tactics and resource allocation. **Strategic management** is used to form the long-term plans for the organization.

Attributes of Information as a Resource

Information shares many characteristics with resources such as coal or steel. For example, information:

- Is useful: Information can be used to solve problems, produce goods or provide services.
- Can be collected: Information can be gathered and stored until it is needed.
- Can be shared: Information may be sold or given away.
- May be modified into other forms: Information can be processed to yield more useable information.
- Is valuable: Information has value because of its utility.
- Can be transported: Information can be transmitted in many ways, including digitally and manually, to nearly anywhere in the world.
- May be abused: Information may be used unethically or illegally.
- Can be protected: Physical, procedural, and technical solutions are available to protect information from unauthorized access.

An organization may find that information is its most valuable resource. Some companies are willing to offer premiums such as special pricing or services in exchange for customers' personal information.

Information is valuable for many reasons. By better understanding their target market, companies are able to develop more efficient marketing strategies. Being able to calculate returns on investments helps organizations to plan for the future. Information can also be sold to other organizations.

SYSTEMS THEORY

A **system** is a construct that achieves defined goals by using resources. Systems can range from a small computer application that tracks household expenses to large corporations that use people, money, natural resources, and machinery to create a product and make a profit.

Characteristics

All systems, from an individual information system to a large multinational corporation, share some common characteristics:

- **Systems function through interrelated subsystems.** A large company, for instance, probably has many departments. Whether it is accounting, marketing, manufacturing or human resources, each department would have its own resources and goals. A word processing application relies on drivers and the computer operating system to interface with the hardware.

- **Systems are made of interdependent elements.** Changing or deleting a subsystem will have an impact throughout the system. Modifying or deleting a system element may lead to a more efficient system.

- **Systems produce change.** Systems must process resources. If the input is the same as the output, you cannot verify that any processing has occurred.

- **Systems have boundaries.** Inputs come from the environment, and outputs go into the environment, but the processing and storage of resources within the system is separate from the environment.

- **Systems can be controlled.** Systems can be regulated to meet changing needs. Some systems may self-correct or update automatically.

- **Systems exist on a continuum of openness and closedness.** Openness refers to the free exchange of resources within the elements of a system. Subsystems that keep resources and make them unavailable to other subsystems are called **closed**.

System Diagrams

Diagramming can help identify a system's characteristics. The **context level data flow diagram**, sometimes called the environmental model, shows the boundaries and the openness/closedness of the entire system.

Context Level Data Flow Diagrams

The context level data flow diagram only shows four types of system components: processes, entities, data flow, and information. **Processes** are actions that result in some sort of change. **Entities** are people, groups, or subsystems that enter or receive data or information. **Data flow** is the movement of data to or from a process or entity. A context level data flow diagram shows only broad groups of information, not specific fields.

A rounded rectangle is used to represent processes. A shaded square represents entities. Data flow is shown by arrows, with the information being passed labeling the arrows.

The following context level data flow diagram shows a simple payroll system. The entities are the employee and the manager. The process is the payroll system, which calculates the employee's weekly pay based on two pieces of information: the hours worked and the hourly rate. The number of hours worked is inputted by the employee while the hourly wage is entered by the manager.

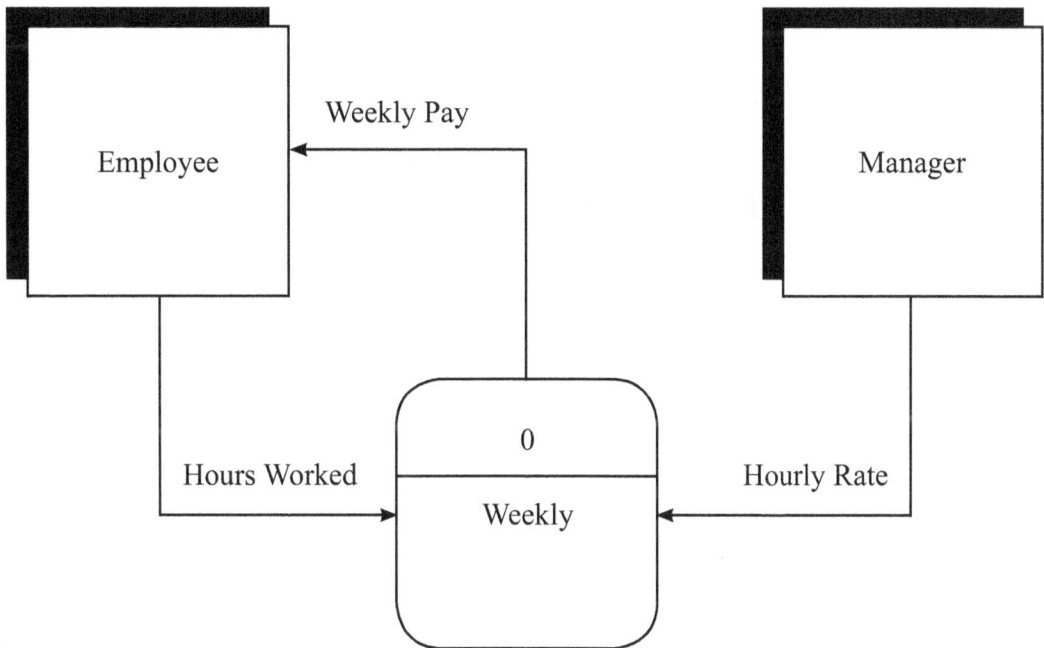

The context level data flow diagram may appear simple, but it tells a lot about the system it diagrams. The context level data flow diagram shows the boundaries for the system. For this payroll system, the employee's weekly pay does not involve what products were sold or how much profit the company showed that week. While those are certainly part of the organizational environment and may be used later to determine if the employee's hourly rate should change, they are not within the boundaries of the weekly payroll system.

The diagram shows that the data that flows into the system is processed. In this example, the hours worked and the hourly rate are used to compute the weekly pay. In addition, the context level data flow diagram illustrates that the system can be controlled by inputting different data.

Level 0 Diagrams

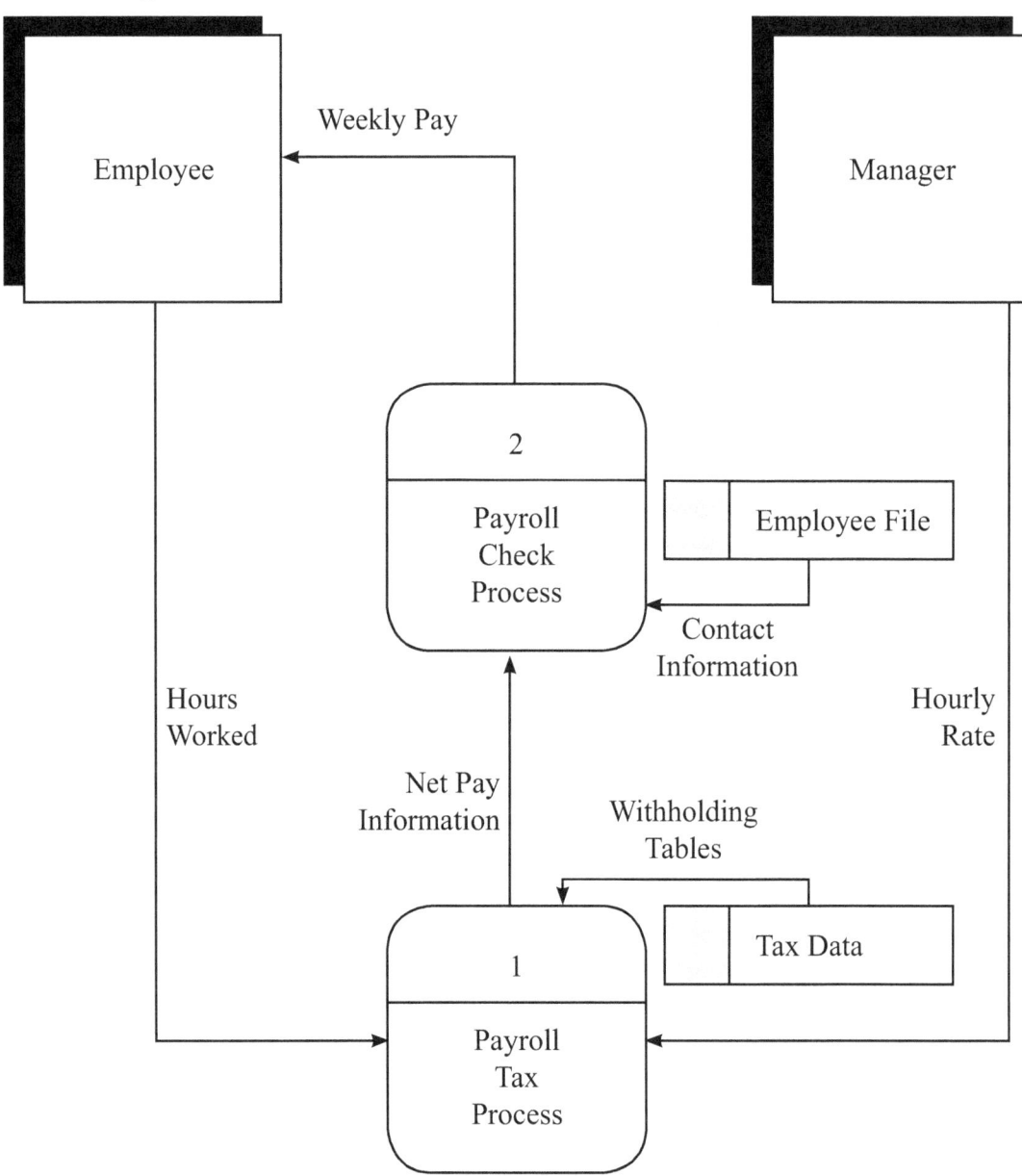

The level 0 ("zero") diagram tells even more about the system. The inputs and outputs from the context level diagram will remain the same for the level 0 and all higher level diagrams.

The level 0 diagram breaks the processes of the context level diagram into greater detail and contains a new element, the file from which data can be retrieved. This is called the data store and is represented by a rectangle with the left side shaded.

Using the example context level diagram, the level 0 diagram shows that the weekly payroll system can be divided into two subsystems: the payroll tax process which uses information from the tax data file to compute net pay and the payroll check process which uses the employee file to cut each employee's weekly paycheck.

A **child diagram** shows the processes of its parent diagram in greater detail. The level 1 diagram is the child diagram of the level 0 diagram. In the example, the level 1 diagram would break the payroll tax and payroll check processes into even more subprocesses. A **primitive process** is one that has not been diagrammed into its subprocesses.

Higher level diagrams can be drawn to show the system in even greater detail. Data flow diagrams should follow these basic rules:

- Each child diagram must have the same inputs and outputs as its parent.
- Data stores and external entities cannot be directly connected to each other. They may only connect to a process.
- For clarity and readability, nine is the maximum number of processes allowed on a data flow diagram. If more than nine processes are required, group some processes in a subsystem and chart them on a separate diagram.
- Except for very rare circumstances in detailed diagrams, avoid creating processing with only one input and one output. This usually means that some data is missing in the diagram or that there is actually no data processing within the system.
- The same data should not flow into and out of a single process.

Relevance to Information Systems

There are two categories of data flow diagrams: logical and physical.

Logical data flow diagrams show how the business operates. The processes represent business activities and the data stores can be any collection of data, including reference manuals and rate schedules.

Physical data flow diagrams, on the other hand, show how the actual or planned system will operate. Processes represent computer and manual applications. Data stores are databases, as well as digital and manual files.

Applying system theory to studying an information system should include constructing both logical and physical data flow diagrams of the operation. Although it is tempting to focus only on the physical data flow diagram, examining the logical model has many benefits:

- System users may be able to understand the logical data flow diagram easier, as it is focused on the business operations.
- Using a logical data flow diagram can help create more stable information systems, as the programmer can more easily identify and work toward the business operations goals rather than building the system around a particular method or technology.
- Business operations change less frequently than physical system elements, so systems built on a logical model may be easier to update.
- Understanding the logical data flow can help the programmer identify inefficiencies and redundancies within the system.

The physical data flow diagram is also important to consider when studying an information system:

- Physical models distinguish between automated and manual processes.
- Physical data flow diagrams can describe processes more completely than logical data flow diagrams.
- Process sequence is more evident on physical diagrams.
- Data stores can be identified as permanent or temporary on physical data flow diagrams.

HARDWARE AND SOFTWARE

History and Evolution of Hardware and Software

For centuries, humans have been using machines to automate tedious calculations. Some historical highlights of the role of hardware and software in information systems include:

- 1623: Wilhelm Schickard crafted the first mechanical calculator.
- 1671: Gottfried Wilhelm von Leibniz introduced a mechanical calculator based on the decimal system.
- 1725-26: Basile Bouchon and Jean-Baptiste Falcon developed a semi-automatic punch card system.
- 1835: Charles Babbage designed the analytic engine, the first programmable calculating machine.
- 1890: The US Census Bureau used punched cards to process data from the census.
- 1900-1930: Mechanical computational machines became popular in the form of cash registers, adding machines, and accounting machines.
- 1946: The ENIAC, a vacuum tube-based digital computer, was built. It weighed about 30 tons.
- 1948: The first portable mechanical calculator was introduced.
- 1951: Forty-six units of the UNIVAC I were constructed, making it the first mass-produced computer.
- 1957: The first high-level programming language, FORTRAN, was released for the IBM 704.
- 1968: The NLS computer interface was introduced. It was the first computer software to use a mouse.
- 1970s: Microcomputers such as the KIM-1, Altair 8800, Apple I, and Commodore PET were marketed to business and home users.
- 1981: Xerox introduced windows, icons, and menus with the "Star" user interface.
- 1984: Apple began selling the Macintosh, the first user interface to feature drop-down menus and a desktop. The system included applications such as a calculator, word processor, and alarm clock.

- 1985: DESQview was introduced, the first program to allow multitasking and windowing with DOS-based applications.
- Commodore released the Amiga, which introduced Workbench, a graphical user interface (GUI) run by AmigaOS.

Throughout the evolution of computers, there has been a constant dance between performance and ease of use. GUIs and other techniques to improve the end-user experience often add overhead which can slow processing time.

Information System Hardware

Information systems often use a variety of hardware components to perform their four key functions. Input devices put data external to the system in a form the system can process. Output devices convert the data internal to the system into a form useful outside of the computer. Storage devices keep the system's data available for processing. The central processing unit (CPU or "processor") is the processing device that carries out the logical and arithmetic instructions from computer programs.

Input Devices

The most common input device is a keyboard. Keyboards may include all the basic keys found on a typewriter as well as a row of special function keys, or may consist of only ten digits and select function keys.

Ergonomics is the study of designing machines for more efficient and comfortable human use. Repetitive strain injuries, including carpal tunnel syndrome, may develop when users perform the same motion for long periods of time. Because repetitive strain injuries are so common among data entry professionals, hardware manufacturers have designed ergonomic keyboards.

Pointing devices are also commonly used for inputting system data. Moving a pointing device controls the cursor on the user's computer screen. The most popular pointing device is a **mouse**, which consists of a ball or optical tracking device housed below a plastic case and controlled by the user's hand and arm motions. A trackball is a ball controlled by the user's fingers. Like a mouse, a **trackball** usually has one or more buttons.

Other pointing devices include **trackpoints** and **trackpads** (or "touch-pads"). Trackpoints are small sticks between the keys of a keyboard. Trackpads are screens that allow the user to control the cursor through the movement of their finger over the screen. Trackpoints and track-pads are most often found on laptop computers.

Less commonly used input devices include:

- Optical scanning devices (for example, barcode readers)
- Magnetic scanning devices (for example, magnetic strip readers)
- Voice input devices (for example, voice recognition applications for telephone systems)
- Camera input devices (for example, digital cameras)

Output Devices

Computer screens are the most common type of output hardware. Screens are useful because they can be updated quickly and easily read. **Pixels** ("picture elements") are the individual dots that form the screen display. Pixels are arranged in patterns to make characters, diagrams, pictures, and other elements.

Screen resolution refers to the number of pixels that can be displayed at one time. The higher the screen resolution, the closer the pixels are together. High screen resolution leads to more finely detailed graphical output. Screen resolution is given in terms of horizontal pixels by vertical pixels. A screen that is 640 by 480 pixels will show lower quality graphics than a screen that is 1280 by 1024 pixels.

There are several types of screens available to computer system users. Cathode ray tube (CRT) monitors are relatively inexpensive and capable of producing finely detailed output. However, they are heavy and take up a lot of space. Liquid crystal display (LCD) flat panel monitors weigh less and have a smaller footprint than their CRT counterparts, but they are more expensive and may be difficult to read in certain lights or at specific angles. Output can also be displayed on a screen projector, which uses LCD technology to display graphics on a viewing screen large enough for several people to see.

A **printer** is a popular choice when a permanent record of output is required. Printers may be classified as **impact** or **nonimpact**, based on how they make images. Impact printers produce an image on paper through striking a ribbon of ink. Dot-matrix printers are impact printers that strike a ribbon of ink with a pattern of pins, creating graphical images on the paper. Dot-matrix printers are very inexpensive, but produce low-quality output.

Nonimpact printers distribute ink on paper through a method that does not involve striking. Two common types of nonimpact printers are inkjet and laser printers. Inkjet printers spray small drops on paper, creating characters and other graphical elements. Laser printers spread toner on a metal drum using a laser. Paper is then rolled over the drum, transferring the image to the paper. Laser printers are usually more expensive than inkjet printers, but often produce higher-quality graphics.

Another way to classify printers is by how many characters they print at one time:
- **Serial printers** print one character at a time. Their printing speed is measured in characters per second (cps).
- **Line printers** print an entire line at one time. Speed is measured in lines per minute (lpm).
- **Page printers** print a page at a time. Speed is measured in pages per minute (ppm).

Other output devices include:
- Plotters
- Voice output devices
- Braille display devices
- Multimedia output devices

Primary Storage

Primary storage, or "internal storage," stores data and processing instructions for programs that are in use. Primary storage devices are integrated circuits ("chips") made from silicon. Primary storage in a computer consists of millions of circuits. Each circuit is either on or off. The pattern of on and off circuits represents data.

The patterns of on/off states within the chips must be converted into **binary representation** in order to be processed by the computer. In binary representation, data is shown using only the digits 1 and 0. The digit 1 represents an on circuit while 0 means an off circuit. Bits, or "binary digits," are another term for the digits 1 and 0. All data within the computer is stored in binary representation. There are several common codes used for binary representation, the *American Standard Code for Information Interchange* (ASCII, pronounced "as key") and the *Extended Binary Coded Decimal Interchange* Code (EBCDIC, pronounced "ebb-see-dik").

ASCII is a seven-bit character system which assigns a number to 128 different characters, including uppercase and lowercase letters and punctuation marks. ASCII is the most accurate and used system for text in American English. Unicode has a much broader character base. It attempts to represent every possible written language and uses 8-, 16-, or 32-bit characters, meaning it can take up much more space than ASCII.

Secondary Storage

Secondary storage, or "auxiliary storage," stores data and programs that can be accessed by the computer, but are not being used at that time.

Organizations have many choices for secondary storage devices, including magnetic disks, optical disks, and mobile devices.

Magnetic Tapes

While magnetic tapes themselves are quite inexpensive, the drives required to record and read tapes can be very costly. Tape drives tend to be slow, and tapes can be vulnerable to environmental damage.

Optical Disks

Optical disks (CD-R and DVD-R) are an inexpensive secondary storage option. However, each disk has limited storage room, so someone must oversee large backup procedures in order to monitor and change disks as needed. Optical disks that are "write only"—that is, the data on them cannot be removed or altered—may be required to comply with some national, state, local, or industrial regulations.

Magnetic Disks

Magnetic or "hard" disks have high storage capacity, making them appropriate for automated backup procedures. They can be saved to and accessed quicker than magnetic tapes. However, they are more expensive per gigabyte of storage than either magnetic tapes or optical disks.

Mobile Devices

Mobile storage devices include thumb drives, flash memory, and pocket drives. The main advantage of using mobile devices is their portability. These devices have very low storage capacity and are quite expensive.

Processing Devices

The central processing unit (CPU) does logical and arithmetic computations using data in primary storage. The circuits in the CPU are divided into two groups: the **arithmetic-logic unit** (ALU) and the **control unit**.

The ALU circuits complete the logical and arithmetic processes. The logical processes an ALU can conduct include:

- Are two values equal?
- Is value x greater than value y?
- Is value x less than value y?

The ALU is able to perform basic mathematical computations:

- Addition
- Subtraction
- Multiplication
- Division

Advanced computations such as square roots or power functions are completed using sequences of basic mathematical functions. Instructions to the CPU arrive in **machine code** (or "machine language"), a low-level programming language. Microprocessors are CPUs that use only one chip. **Multiprocessors** involve many CPUs.

These chip capabilities constantly change. Moore's law is based on an observation made by Gordon Moore in 1965. He showed that since the invention of the integrated circuit, the number of transistors per square inch, or the data density, had approximately doubled every year. Moore's law is his prediction that this trend would continue. Because in recent years the trend has slowed slightly, the current definition of Moore's law is that the data density will double every 18 months.

John von Neumann was a Hungarian scientist and mathematician in the early 20th century responsible for developing the Von Neumann architecture for computers. The Von Neumann architecture was the first theory to allow for a working memory, or stored program system, which we refer to today as RAM. The Von Neumann architecture includes five elements: CPU, input, output, working memory, and permanent memory.

Information System Software

Software (or "programs") tell the computer how to interact with the storage, input, output, and processing hardware. Information systems consist of applications, which perform the functions required of the system.

Software Development

Natural languages are sets of rules, words, and symbols that allow communication between people. English, Spanish, and Tagalog are natural languages.

Programming languages, like natural languages, are sets of rules, words, and symbols. Programming languages allow users to communicate with the computer. Applications are written using programming languages. There are many different types of programming languages, each with their own strengths and weaknesses. When choosing a language to write an application with, the programmer considers:

- **Availability:** What languages are available?
- **Appropriateness:** Is the language appropriate for the type of program?
- **Popularity:** Are programmers who know the language available for maintenance and updates?
- **Ease of use:** How hard is it to write in the language? How much time will be required?

First Generation Programming Languages

Machine language is considered the first generation of programming languages. Machine language consists of **operation codes** for simple logical and mathematical processes and operands that name what data is involved in the process.

Machine language is **machine dependent**. That is, different types of computers have their own machine language, which may be different from the language used by other computers.

All higher-level programming languages must be translated into machine language before the computer can understand the instructions. Machine code is written in binary, with only the digits 0 and 1 representing all the operands and operations codes. Although very efficient, machine language is difficult to learn, write, debug, and update.

Second Generation Programming Languages

Assembly languages are second generation languages. Assembly languages replace binary codes with simple symbols and words, such as SUBTRACT and Y. An **assembler** translates assembly language into machine code.

Like machine language, assembly code is efficient, but difficult to use. Assembly code is machine-dependent.

Third Generation Programming Languages

By the 1950s, programming languages were developed that were closer to natural languages. This third generation of programming languages included FORTRAN and COBOL.

Like assembly language, third generation languages must be translated into machine language in order to affect the computer processing. One way this is accomplished is by using a **compiler**. A compiler is a program which translates an entire program into machine code, then executes the instructions. Another method of translating is through the use of an **interpreter**. An interpreter translates individual instructions, allowing them to be executed individually by the computer.

Third generation languages are easier to learn and maintain than lower level languages, but they are not as efficient. Third generation languages are machine-independent.

There are two main types of third generation languages: traditional and object-oriented (O-O). Programmers using traditional languages create lists of instructions for processing data. The data used in the program may come from the computer's data files or from a database. Traditional programming languages include BASIC, COBOL, C, and FORTRAN.

Object-oriented programming combines the processing instructions with the data. The combination of data plus instructions is called an object. After an object has been created, it can be reused by other programs. O-O languages include C++, C# ("C-Sharp"), and Visual BASIC.

Fourth Generation Programming Languages

Fourth generation languages (4GL) make it easier to write complicated mathematical processes. They provide simplified methods for coding complex statistical, graphical, and logical operations. 4GLs may include features such as:

- Query language: allows users to find data that meets certain criteria within a database.
- Report generators: facilitate production and formation of reports.
- Form designers: allow the programmer to build forms for the input and output of data.
- Application generations: allow the programmer to combine elements to make an attractive and productive computer application.

Operating Systems

An operating system consists of several programs that oversee control of the computer hardware. The operating system has three main functions:

- Process management
- Resource management
- Data management

The process management function involves starting, stopping, and monitoring programs. The resource management function involves assigning resources to each program that is running. Resources include access to primary and secondary storage, and to input and output devices. The data management function controls the transfer of data between primary storage and hardware.

Operating systems may include many features, including:

- **Virtual memory:** The ability to divide large programs into parts within secondary storage and only load one part at a time into primary storage. This allows programs to use less primary memory than if they were loaded completely.
- **Multitasking:** The ability to execute more than one program at a time.
- **Multiple-User:** Allows more than one user to access the computer simultaneously.
- **Interactivity:** Allows users to process data as it is inputted, rather than having to wait for all of the data to be prepared.

Although an operating system includes many programs, often only one program is running at all times—the **supervisor**. The supervisor determines if other operating system programs are needed. If they are, the supervisor loads them into primary storage and signals them to start.

Booting is the act of loading the supervisor into primary storage. Once the computer has "booted up," the user is able to tell the computer what to do through the **user interface**. Depending on the operating system, the user interface may be text-based, menu-based, icon-based, or a combination of these.

Text-based user interfaces require the user to enter words or phrases as commands in order to start programs. A menu-based system allows the user to choose commands from a list. An icon-based operating system allows the user to select small pictures that represent processes or applications. A **graphical user interface (GUI)** is an interface that uses icons and/or menus.

Groupware

Groupware, or collaborative software, is the name given to programs or software which allow multiple people to access and use an application to achieve a common goal. In other words, groupware is software which allows people to work together. There are many reasons that a company may wish to employ groupware. One of the biggest reasons is because of geographic issues. If a company has employees in different locations, they may employ some form of groupware to make the work more effective and efficient. Even if employees are in the same locations, groupware may be used simply to enhance communication in general.

There are three basic types or uses of groupware: communication, conferencing, and collaboration. Communication groupware is used to facilitate (or increase) unstructured communication among employees. This type of groupware includes emails, faxes, voicemail, and other forms of communication. Conferencing is any type of program which is used to facilitate structured communication, such as meetings. For example, videoconferencing, online chat, and instant messaging are all types of conferencing groupware. Collaborative groupware allows for employees to truly work together on projects and achieve goals, as opposed to just aiding in the communication process. Some examples include online calendaring, knowledge support systems, workflow systems, and others.

Information Architecture Terminology

As organizations deal with increasing amounts of information, there is a growing demand for systems that are both fast and easy to use. Information architecture refers to the way information is grouped and navigated within a system. Information architecture is important since inefficient design can lead to user frustration and long access times.

When building an information system, the architecture can be approached in two main ways: top-down or bottom-up.

Top-down information architecture occurs when the broad functioning of the system is considered first. Next, the high-level structure is determined. Finally, detailed attribute lists are constructed and relationships between entities are defined.

Bottom-up information architecture considers the details of individual entities first. Next, the designer considers specific functions of the system. Finally, the high-level organization is analyzed and defined.

Information architecture projects usually employ both techniques. A system that is constructed completely bottom-up may be detailed and well-organized but not meet the organization's needs. On the other hand, a system built completely top-down may lack diverse functionality and fail to accommodate future growth.

There are many tools used in the information architecture process, including:

- **Site maps:** High-level diagrams that represent the hierarchy of a system.
- **Personas:** Written studies of the end users of the system, used to determine system and user needs.
- **Prototypes:** System models that show the functionality of a system, used to get user feedback before building the actual system.
- **Content matrix:** Defines what information needs to be available at each interface level of the system, and how the different interface levels should relate.

There are many facets to the architecture of an information system:

- **Interface design:** Techniques used to make the user experience easier. The user experience includes such functions as inputting data, asking for information, and viewing information.
- **Functional specifications:** The list of tasks the system must be able to perform.
- **User needs:** Goals external to the functional specifications, often based on personas. User needs may include cues, interfaces that can be personalized, verbal commands, and tutorials. User needs are what the system needs to have in order to be accepted by the users.
- **System objectives:** Long-term goals for the system, for example, to improve long range marketing strategies. System objectives are not concrete specifications, but they do help the architect determine what information may be needed in the future.

SYSTEM LEVEL

Information systems can be divided into four general categories: individual, workgroup, organizational, and interorganizational.

 Individual Information Systems

Individual information systems are those that accept inputted data from one user, then store, process, and output the information for the same user. They are often used to improve a single user's ability to contribute to the organization through managing, analyzing, and presenting information. They can also be used to assist the user in solving problems.

Managing Data

Individual information systems may store data in individual files or in databases. Databases are usually preferred because they make searching for and retrieving specific data easier. Individuals can interact with databases in a number of ways. They may create databases, populate the database with the initial data, access data that is stored in the database, update records, create new entries, delete data, or edit information.

Analyzing Data

After users access stored data, they may need to analyze the data. Spreadsheets can be helpful in this step.

To use spreadsheet software, the user must enter data into a **worksheet**. Worksheets are tables where each cell has a unique identifier—its row and column positions. Most spreadsheet packages come preprogrammed with common accounting and statistics functions. Users can input other equations if needed.

When the value in a cell is changed, all calculations based on that cell are automatically updated. This feature makes the spreadsheet especially valuable for examining complicated "what if" scenarios. For example, "What would happen if revenues increased by 10%, salaries increased by 6%, and the cost of operation increased by 8% next year?"

A well-integrated individual information system may combine the data management and analysis functions. This occurs when data from the database automatically populates the spreadsheet. In other words, the output from the management phase becomes the input for the analysis phase. Integration between applications can make the movement of data between subsystems quicker and more accurate.

Presenting Information

Users may have to share the information revealed through data analysis. Individual information systems often include applications to facilitate presenting data in text form, graphically, in presentations, through publication, and in multimedia formats.

Text Presentations

Text presentations of information include letters, memos, and reports. They are often created using word processing software that allows the user to create a document, enter characters, format the text, edit the information, and print the document.

Graphical Presentations

Sometimes it is more appropriate to convey information using charts, graphs, or diagrams. Graphics software includes general applications as well as more programs used specifically for making flow charts, blueprints, drawings, or graphs.

Computer-aided design (CAD) software is a subset of graphics software. CAD software allows engineers, architects, surveyors, and builders to create, edit, and analyze maps, designs, and blueprints.

Some graphics software is integrated with presentation software, allowing the user to create video presentations or slide shows. Word processors and spreadsheets often include simple graphics functions, or can be integrated with more sophisticated graphics programs.

Publishing Information

By using desktop publishing software, information may be presented through reports, newsletters, brochures, pamphlets, or books. Desktop publishing applications offer some word processing and graphics functions as well as powerful formatting and layout options.

Multimedia Publications

Multimedia presentations may convey information through any combination of the following: sound, text, animation, video, or graphics. These presentations are usually created using authoring software, which allows the user to weave together previously prepared elements.

Problem Solving

Individual information systems can also function as management information systems by helping users find solutions to business issues.

Using information systems to solve problems involves five major steps:

1) Recognizing the problem
2) Developing a solution
3) Implementing the solution
4) Testing the solution
5) Documenting the result

Recognizing the Problem

In order to solve a problem, the IS user must first understand and define the issues. Studying and defining the problem should continue until there are sufficient specifications for developing a solution.

The problem definition should include:

- The output that will need to be produced by the solution.
- The format the output will need to take.
- The data available for input into the solution system.
- The calculations needed to transform the available input into the required output.
- Any other procedures required of the solution.

Developing a Solution

Throughout the problem definition and solution development phases, IS users should keep in mind the applications available. Complex problems may require a combination of tools. Some common problem-solving software available to individual IS users are summarized in the table below.

COMMON INDIVIDUAL I.S. APPLICATIONS		
Software Type	*Useful For:*	*Usually Not a Good Choice For:*
Database	Storing, updating, or retrieving large amounts of data Organizing different groups of related data	Complex computations Storing small, simple lists "What if" scenarios
Spreadsheet	Storing and ordering small, simple lists Complex numerical computations "What if" scenarios	Storing large or complicated sets of data
Word Processing	Storing, editing and formatting small, simple lists Presenting text-based information	Graphic-intensive publications Numerical computations
Graphics	Creating graphic-intense presentations Editing or manipulating graphics	Text-based presentations Designing publications
Desktop Publishing	Designing publications	Editing or manipulating graphics
Authoring	Creating multimedia presentations	Editing or manipulating graphics Presenting text-based information Designing publications
Specialized Applications	Tasks not addressed by general individual IS applications	Tasks that can be completed easier using general productivity software

The solution design process involves outlining the steps needed to yield the required output.

Implementing the Solution

Once a solution game plan has been written, the user enters the input into the selected application and steps through the outline developed in the previous phase. Errors in the solution design or misunderstanding of the problem may come to light at this point, and the user may have to redefine the problem or develop a different solution.

Testing the Solution

Testing is the process of locating errors in a software implementation. The testing phase involves four steps:

1) Create sample input data.
2) Using the sample data, work out the solution to the problem by hand.
3) Input the sample data into the software implementation. Run the implementation.
4) Compare the output from step 2 with the output from step 3.

If the outputs are not identical, the user must review the software implementation and possible design for logical errors.

Documenting the Result

Once the user is confident in the accuracy of the software implementation, the final step is to create a written description of the solution.

User documentation includes instructions for using the software implementation to solve the defined problem. This includes how to input the data and how to retrieve the output. User documentation should include the kind of output users should expect and the meanings of any special terms.

Developer documentation is meant for the person who created the software implementation. It describes the problem, the solution design, and the implementation. Developer documentation is valuable if the implementation later needs to be serviced or updated.

 Workgroup Information Systems

A workgroup information system is used by several individuals who share a common function or goal, such as a project team or business department. The users may work on separate computers connected by a **local area network** (LAN), a **wide area network** (WAN), or the internet.

Group collaboration allows people within an organization to coordinate, share ideas, comment on different aspects of a project, and transfer documents, images, and designs.

If the group members are not in the same place at the same time, however, meetings can be inefficient and unproductive.

Communication systems can help groups function even if the members are separated. Forms of group communication include:

- **Audio communication**, usually by telephone.
- **Visual communication**, often by video conferencing.
- **Document communication** ("data communication"), the transfer of written information by electronic file transfer, electronic messaging, traditional mail, or fax.

Groupware is a general term for collaborative software used with networked computers. Groupware can be designed to work over LANs, WANs or the internet. Groupware applications differ in time, place and form characteristics. The main types of groupware are:

- **Electronic Messaging** – Electronic messaging is a specific type of document communication between group members at different locations and times. Email, instant messaging, and chat are forms of electronic messaging.

- **Information Sharing** – Information sharing is a type of document, audio, and/or visual communication between group members separated by location or time. Through information sharing, members can review and revise information documents such as charts, spreadsheets, videos, and text.

- **Document Conferencing** – Document (or "data") conferencing is related to information sharing, but used when group members are available to work at the same time. They may still be in different locations. Through **whiteboard conferencing**, group members are able to view the same document on different screens. Users can comment on the document and all group members see the comments immediately. With **application conferencing**, users see the same document at the same time through the application program. Comments or changes made by one user are seen immediately by other members of the group.

- **Audioconferencing** – Audioconferences through a computer network or the telephone allow one or more group member to talk about a project at the same time, even if they are in different locations. Audioconferencing is a form of audio communication.

- **Videoconferencing** – Videoconferencing occurs between members at the same time but in different locations. This type of groupware allows members to see each other while discussing projects.

- **Electronic Conferencing** – Electronic conferencing is a combination of videoconferencing and whiteboard conferencing, allowing users separated by distance to discuss particular documents while seeing each other's facial expressions.

- **Electronic Meeting Support** – Electronic meeting systems (EMS) support meetings between group members who are in the same place at the same time. EMS may function between separate work stations within one room or by one central computer in a wired meeting room. Participants of an electronic meeting can key comments in from their workstation or laptop to be distributed to other group members in the meeting room.
- **Group Calendaring and Scheduling** – Group calendaring and scheduling applications aid team coordination. This type of software allows users to create individual calendars. This kind of software makes scheduling a meeting easy—a group member selects the users that need to attend and the group calendaring and scheduling system finds available times.
- **Workflow Management** – Workflow management software allows group members to schedule chunks of a large project. Users can see who is responsible for different tasks and review scheduling to make the project workflow more efficient.

Organizational Information Systems

An organizational information system is one that includes people from several groups. Also called "enterprise information systems," organizational information systems are often based on mainframe computer or a **wide area network** (WAN).

For many organizations, a transaction processing system (TPS) is the main information system used. TPSs share four main goals:

- To store records about the organization (for example, inventory information).
- To process transactions (sales, rentals, purchases).
- To update the organizational records based on transactions.
- To produce required outputs.

TPSs often have controls to help ensure that data is accurate and complete. Common TPS controls include:

- **Control Totals** – Comparison of data before and after processing to locate possible errors.
- **Audit Trails** – Tracing data through a system, forward (from input to output) or backwards (from output to input).

- **Backup Procedures** – Storing copies of important data on external media.
- **Recover Procedures** – Recreating system information after a failure by using data from backup media.

Besides TPSs, organizational information systems commonly include order entry, billing, accounts receivable, inventory control, purchasing, accounts payable, payroll, and general ledger systems.

Order Entry Systems

Order entry systems accept order information from customers (input function), check the business inventory and customer credit (processing function), create the sales order (output function), store the customer information, and update the inventory data file (storage function).

Billing Systems

A billing system uses sales order data (input function) to tally the order amount (processing function), produces an invoice (output function), and updates customer and inventory data files (storage function).

Accounts Receivable Systems

An accounts receivable system accepts invoice and customer payment information (input function). It then calculates the new balance due (processing function) and produces a billing statement (output function). The system also updates accounts receivable and customer data files (storage function).

Inventory Control Systems

Inventory control systems take delivery and order data (input function) and calculate new inventory data, as well as check for low quantities (processing function). These systems produce inventory reorder and value reports (output function) and update inventory data files (storage function).

Purchasing Systems

A purchasing system determines the best vendors (processing function) using inventory reorder data such as sales policies, performance information, price, and delivery time (input function) to yield purchase orders (output function). The system updates and stores inventory and supplier data (storage function).

Accounts Payable Systems

Accounts payable systems produce accounts payable reports and supplier payment checks (output function) by using purchase orders and supplier invoices (input function) to compute total accounts payable (processing function) and update accounts payable and supplier data (storage function).

Payroll Systems

Payroll systems use employee work records (input function) to compute payroll totals (processing function) and print paychecks and payroll reports (output function). Payroll systems also store employee work and contact information (storage function).

General Ledger Systems

The general ledger system uses expense, revenue, asset, and liability data (input function) to calculate financial data (processing function) and produce statements (output function). The system maintains an updated general ledger (storage function).

Other business information systems include accounting, financial, marketing, manufacturing, and human resource information systems.

For many organizations, information systems require the coordination of many departments. **Enterprise resource planning** (ERP) systems store all business data within a single database, letting users across the organization access and update integrated information.

Interorganizational Information Systems

Interorganizational information systems connect groups of computers in different organizations using an interorganizational network.

Interorganizational information systems can be intimately related to organizational information systems. Accounts payable, accounts receivable, and purchasing systems, for example, often include business-to-business (B2B) transactions. If two businesses form an ongoing relationship, then establishing a shared **interorganizational information system** (IOS) automates order processing and payment functions.

IOSs depend on each business transmitting data in a form that the other business can understand. In order to keep the data secure, encryption protocols may be used.

Businesses may function in an IOS as either a sponsor or a participant. The **sponsor** establishes and maintains the system. The **participant** uses the system.

An electronic data interchange (EDI) system allows businesses to transfer data. Electronic data interchange (EDI) is the exchange of documents electronically (i.e., from computer to computer) between businesses. The important thing to remember about EDI is that it goes beyond communication (such as email or letters). It refers to situations in which electronic business documents replace physical copies. This occurs with receipts, invoices, shipping information and notices, designs, and other documents. EDI occurs through predetermined protocols. EDI allows data to be transmitted faster and more accurately than traditional, paper-based methods, often reducing the cost of business. However, there are both organizational and technical problems with EDI. Both businesses must agree to participate and cooperate, and hardware and software must be compatible. An electronic funds transfer (EFT) system is a specialized EDI system used to transfer money between organizations.

DATABASE MANAGEMENT

Database applications use input in the form of data files and user queries to produce reports—for example, a list of all customers that purchased a particular product in the last year. Database management involves designing and updating databases to most efficiently perform the input, processing, storage, and output processes.

Data Models

Data models graphically represent the composition of and relationship between data in a database system. Three common types of data models are the entity-relationship (E-R) model, semantic object model, and relational model.

Entity-Relationship Model

E-R models, developed by Peter Chen in 1976, look at four elements: entities, relationships, attributes, and identifiers.

Entities

In E-R models, an **entity** is something that can be identified and tracked within the system environment. For a retail store, an entity may be a piece of merchandise, an employee, an order, or a cash register. All similar entities can be considered as a single unity—an **entity class**. A particular entity within an entity class is called an **instance**. For example, all of the accounts in a bank can be grouped together as an entity class. Account number 1234 is an instance within that class.

Relationships

The association between two or more entities is called a **relationship**. If the relation is between entire entity classes, it is called a **relationship class**. If it is only between certain instances, it is called a relationship instance. The **degree** of a relationship is the number of entities involved. **Binary relationships** are common in systems. Binary relationships occur between two entities. In other words, they are of degree 2. The following chart describes the degrees of some sample relationships.

DEGREES OF SAMPLE RELATIONSHIPS		
Relationship Description	*Entities Involved*	*Degree*
A company hires an architect and a contractor to construct a building	Client Architect Contractor	3
One person owns several residences	Person Residence	2
One teacher teaches several classes	Teacher Classes	2
Each student in a class is assigned a study partner	Students	2

Attributes

An entity's characteristics are called its **attributes**. Consider a piece of merchandise in a retail store. It may have some of the following attributes: size, price, color, and manufacturer. Like entities, relationships can have attributes.

Identifiers

Certain incidences within entity groups may share many attributes. For instance, there may be many shirts in a store that are the same color. In order to be tracked, an individual incidence needs an attribute that is unique. The attribute that describes a particular incidence and no other is called the **identifier**. Serial numbers, social security numbers, and account numbers are common identifiers in information systems. Some systems may require more than one attribute to uniquely identify an incidence. These identifiers are called **composite identifiers**.

Creating E-R Diagrams

Diagrams may take a variety of forms. The standard is to use rectangles to show entity classes and diamonds to show relationships.

Binary relationships are the most common type of relationship in information systems. They can be divided into three types. If a single instance of an entity class is related to a single instance of another class, the relationship is called **1:1** ("one to one"). If one instance of an entity class can be related to many instances of another class, the relationship is called **1:N** ("one to many" or "one to N"). If many instances of each class can be involved in the relationship, the relationship is called **N:M** ("many to many" or "N to M").

The maximum cardinality of the relationship is labeled inside the diamond. The **maximum cardinality** is the maximum number of entity instances that can be involved on each side of the relationship.

The following table shows the type and maximum cardinality of some binary relationships.

EXAMPLE RELATIONSHIPS		
Relationship Description	*Type of Binary Relationship*	*Maximum Cardinality*
Each apartment in a building has a phone line.	1:1	1:1
A high school student can take up to six classes a semester.	1:N	1:6
A person can belong to several civic organizations, and each organization can have several members.	N:M	N:M

In an E-R diagram, ellipses represent attributes. The ellipses are connected to the entities they describe by lines.

The following E-R diagrams illustrate the relationship between apartments and telephone lines.

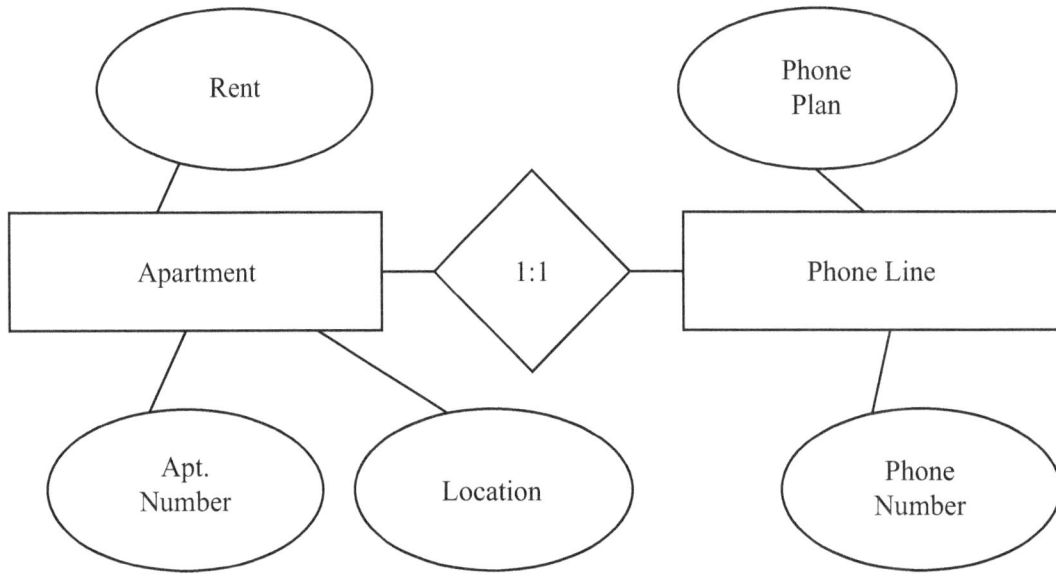

Semantic Object Model

Systems can be thought of as a collection of semantic, or meaningful, objects. Like entities in the E-R model, semantic objects represent identifiable things, have attributes, and can be grouped into classes. Unlike entities, semantic objects can have attributes that describe their relationship to other objects. For example, the semantic object EMPLOYEE may have attributes such as "name," "Social Security number," and "position." It may also have the object attribute "department," which links the object to another semantic object, DEPARTMENT. DEPARTMENT may include attributes such as "address," "office number," and "fax number" that describe the department where the employee works.

Relational Model

The relational model is a more general way of representing information systems, especially databases.

Relational models are based on relations—two-dimensional tables of data. The rows of a relation are called **tuples** and the columns are called **attributes**. Each cell of the relation must be a single value, and all cells in an attribute must be of the same kind (for example, telephone number, name, or transaction number). Each attribute must have a unique name. Each tuple must be unique, and the order of the tuples and attributes must be insignificant.

Any table that is a relation is not necessarily an efficient database design. **Normalization** is a process of breaking down relations to make better structures. Normalization optimizes database performance by reducing data redundancy.

 Hierarchy of Data

When referring to data, a hierarchy (or "tree") is a structure where the only relationships are one-to-many. Each element in a hierarchy is called a node. The relationships between the nodes are called branches. The element immediately above a node is called its parent. The nodes immediately below and related to a node are called its children. The root of the tree is the top node, termed "node 1." Nodes with the same parent are called siblings.

The following diagram shows a data hierarchy.

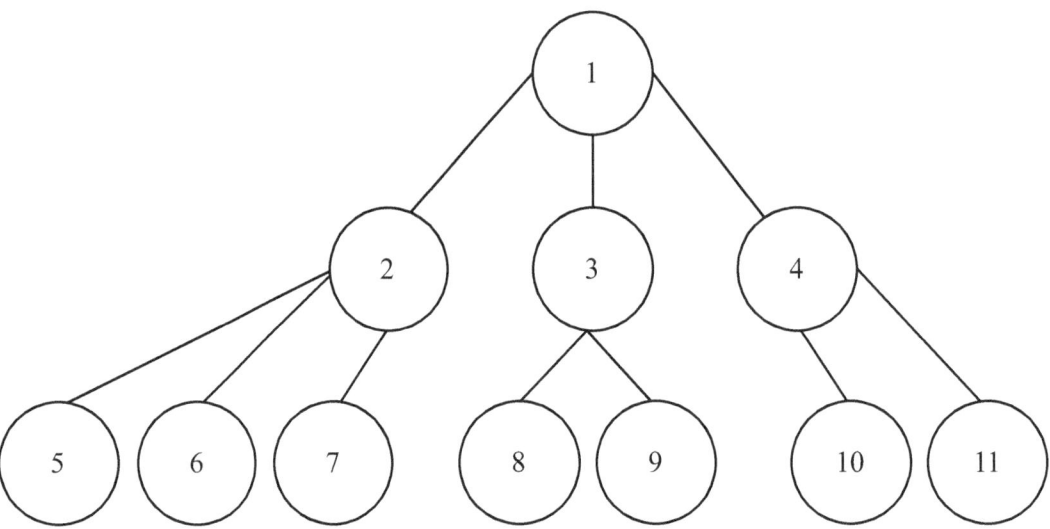

 Organizing Data

A **field** represents a single piece of information. Related fields are grouped together in a **record**. Records are grouped together in a file. For example, the fields "name," "price," "color," and "number in stock" make a product's record. The records of all of the products that a business supplies compose a file.

A **database** consists of related files. A product database, for example, may include the product file and the customer file, as well as the relationships between the two files—for example, what products each customer bought.

 Data Query

Queries are used to drive the processing function of the database system to output specific information. Queries can be expressed in several ways, including by example, by form, or through structured query language (SQL).

An SQL projection requires the keywords SELECT and FROM. SELECT tells the system what attributes the user requires as output. An asterisk (*) in the SELECT command indicates that all attributes from the relation should be returned. FROM designates the relation that will provide the input.

In addition to the required keywords, a projection can specify criteria for output using the WHERE command. The ORDER BY keyword is used to tell the system how the output should be arranged. In the ORDER BY command, ASC means "ascending" and DESC means "descending."

The following SQL query would yield a list of all employees hired after January 1, 2005. The list would be in alphabetical order by last name.

SELECT   LastName, FirstName
FROM   EMPLOYEE
WHERE   HireDate>1/1/2005
ORDER BY   LastName ASC

SQL has a few built-in mathematical functions such as COUNT, SUM and AVG (average).

Data Update

Although many database systems have forms for inserting, deleting, or editing records, data updates can also be performed using SQL. The syntax INSERT INTO… VALUES is used to place new records.

INSERT   INTO EMPLOYEE
              (EmployeeNumber, LastName, FirstName, HireDate, Department)
              VALUES (156, 'Doe', 'John', 1/1/2004, 'Advertising')

Records can be deleted from the database using the command
              DELETE… WHERE.

DELETE   EMPLOYEE
WHERE   EMPLOYEE.EmployeeNumber = 156

The UPDATE… SET… WHERE command is used to edit a data record.
              UPDATE   EMPLOYEE

SET   LastName = 'Smith'
WHERE   EmployeeNumber = 170

The insert, delete, and edit functions can be used on single records or sets of data. If a business were to lay off the entire advertising department, for example, the database administrator might use the following SQL projection:

DELETE   EMPLOYEE
WHERE   EMPLOYEE.Department = 'Advertising'

 DBMS

Database Management Systems (DBMS) are used to help organize and analyze the information stored in a database. The user simply inputs a query, which indicates the information that they want displayed, and the system will go through the files in the database to find the answer. For example, libraries that have online catalogs are a type of DBMS. The user, or the person searching for a book, inputs a query, such as the name of the book, and the system searches through the library's records to return all the results that fit the query.

DBMSs can work in many different ways. Two structures through which DBMSs can organize data are the relational model and the hierarchical model. The hierarchical model was one of the earliest models used in databases. It organizes information into parent-child relationships, essentially making a tree of information where one category leads to other categories which leads to other categories. They can only be connected by going up through the levels. Because of this inefficiency, relational database structures are now more commonly used. The relational model organizes data into tables.

Each table would have a column with the primary information, and any other relevant information that goes along with it. The information is connected to all other tables that contain similar information (which would then also have additional or different information), creating a web rather than a tree.

The problem that naturally arises with relational models is redundancy. Information may be placed in multiple tables or areas which just takes up storage and makes organization more difficult. Because of this problem the practice of normalization evolved. The goal of normalization is to reduce redundancy and ensure that information stored on tables is actually relevant. There are many different levels of organization which build on one another. These range from the First Normal Form (1NF), which includes deleting duplicate information on a table, to the Fourth Normal Form (4NF).

ANALYSIS AND DESIGN OF SYSTEMS

 ## *Traditional Systems Development Life Cycle (SDLC)*

The traditional systems development life cycle (SDLC) includes five phases:

- Planning
- Analysis
- Design
- Implementation
- Maintenance

Planning

To begin the SDLC, someone must decide that a new information system is required. In the planning phase, the symptoms and problems of the current system are identified, separated, and documented. This documentation will help in the later design of the new system.

Often, the planning phase includes a feasibility analysis, where an analyst considers the technical, operational, and economic constraints of developing a new system.

- **Technical feasibility:** Can the system be developed on the current hardware and software?
- **Operational feasibility:** Will the users accept and use a new system?
- **Economical feasibility:** Can the operation afford to institute a new system? Will the benefits of a new system be worth the cost?

If the feasibility study determines that the company does not have the resources to build a new system, or that employees will not accept a new system, the project may end in the planning phase. However, if the organization seems ready to develop a new information system, the SDLC continues to the analysis phase.

Analysis

In the analysis phase, the analyst uses the problems and causes documented in the planning phase to determine what the new system must do.

The first step in system analysis is to document the current system. In order to do this, the analyst must:

- Gather copies of all forms and documents used in the system.
- For computer systems, identify inputs used by the system, processes carried out by the system, databases and files within the system, and output screens and reports generated by the system.
- Interview users to define what the current system accomplishes.
- Prepare written documentation of the current system.

After the current system has been documented, the analyst must determine what the user needs from the new system. This is usually accomplished through interviewing users. User requirements should be written that address the problems identified in the planning phase.

After the user needs are defined, the analyst creates the conceptual design of the system, which addresses what the new system will have to do in order to satisfy the user requirements. The analyst then examines different ways to approach the conceptual design. The analyst must estimate the costs of, and compare the advantages and disadvantages of several different hardware and software alternatives. Some of the choices the analyst may have include:

- Should the system use packaged software, modified software, customer software developed in-house, or custom software created outside the organization ("outsourced")?
- Will the system use in-house hardware or hardware from outside the organization?
- Will the system use personal, multiple-user, or networked computers?

After analyzing the information, the best choice is selected and justified in writing. Some analysts break the analysis phase into two distinct steps: defining the system requirements and analyzing the system needs.

During the analysis phase, the analyst may determine that the current system meets all the user requirements and that a new system is not needed. In this case, the SDLC ends at the analysis phase. If the analyst determines that a new system is needed, the project will proceed to the design phase.

Design

The analysis phase defines what the system will do. The design phase details how the system will meet its objectives. The process focuses on answering fundamental questions about the input, output, storage, and processing functions of the system.

Designing Input

During the design process, the analyst must determine:

- What form will the inputted information be in?
- How will it be entered—by keyboard, mouse, optical reader, or some other device?
- What will screens and forms look like?
- Who will be involved in inputting information?
- What input procedures will be used?

An information system depends on the input of high-quality information. Well-designed input screens and forms should be accurate, effective, easy to use, consistent, attractive, and simple.

Input forms, whether on paper or on the computer, usually include some or all of these main sections:

- **Heading:** The title of the form.
- **Identification:** Basic information about the topic of the form. The input screen for a student registration form, for instance, may include the student's name, address, and Social Security number in the identification section.
- **Instructions:** Directions for completing the body of the form.
- **Body:** Section where information can be added or modified. With a computer-based form, some sections of the body may be completed automatically.
- **Totals:** Numerical totals of rows in the body. With a computerized form, the totals are often calculated automatically as the body of the form is completed.
- **Verification:** Usually a signature line or a "submit" button.
- **Comments:** Space for additional information not in the identification or body sections.

In the following example form, the heading section is located at the top and labeled "Student Registration Form." The identification section follows, with basic information about the student. Next, the instruction section details how to complete the form. Below this is the body of the form. If this were a computer-based form, the "Course Name," "Credit Hours," and "Cost" fields could be updated automatically as the user inputted the CIDNs. The total section follows the body. The signature fields comprise the verification section. The last part of the example is the comments section.

Student Registration Form

Student Information

Name   ID Number
Address   Major
            Grad. Date

Enter Course ID Number (CIDN) for Each Class

CIDN	Course Name	Credit Hours	Cost

Total

Student Signature

Advisor Signature

Additional Comments

The order of the sections may vary, and some forms may not include all sections. Computer-based forms may divide sections into linked screens.

Input forms should be easy to complete. Basic guidelines for designing a user-friendly form include:

- Design forms to flow from left to right and top to bottom, as English is read.
- All fields in an input document should be clearly labeled ("captioned").
- Make sure the forms are uncluttered.
- Include adequate room for each field.
- Group fields that relate to each other close together.

Designing Output

The goals of the design process, with regard to system output, include answering the following questions:

- How will the outputted information be formatted?
- Will it be displayed on paper or on a monitor?
- What will reports look like?
- Who will have access to outputted information?

Users will not accept a system that does not output meaningful and useful information. A good output:

- Has a purpose
- Is meaningful to the user
- Provides information that is neither too broad nor too detailed
- Is available exclusively to the people who need it
- Is timely
- Is displayed on effective media

A system may need to provide both internal and external outputs. **Internal outputs** are distributed within the organization. A product performance report sent to decision makers is an internal output. **External outputs** are sent to people outside of the organization. Customer bills are external outputs.

Information may be outputted on paper, on a display screen, on digital storage media, as email, or as audio output. An analyst decides on the optimal output method for a piece of information by evaluating many variables, including:

- User needs
- Cost
- Speed
- Interactivity
- Number of users needing the information
- Size of the information
- Purpose of the information
- Length of time the information must remain available
- How frequently the information will be accessed
- Hardware and software available
- Security level of the information

Computer-based outputs can offer more flexible design options. For example, outputs with large amounts of information can be reported on separate, linked screens. By including interactive search functions, users can pull up specific information quickly.

Designing Data Storage

When designing data storage for the system, the analyst needs to decide:

- Will data be stored in files or in a database?
- What media will be used for secondary storage?
- How will records, files, and databases be organized?

Records can be stored in either files or databases. When deciding whether to use a file or a database, the analyst considers the advantages and disadvantages of each type of processing for the system. In general, databases are able to provide more accurate and current data because there is less duplication. In addition, databases facilitate the processing of large groups of data. System applications may rely on the structure of data files, but databases can be reorganized and updated without affecting the system's programs.

On the other hand, databases tend to be much more expensive to use than data files. Because of the lack of duplication, data stored in databases may be more vulnerable than data stored in files. Basing a system on a database can be more complex and require more expertise than building one based on data files.

If an analyst chooses to use data files, there are many types which may be incorporated into an information system:

- **Master files:** Relatively permanent records about entities, usually stored as indexed or index-sequential files. Master files may be part of a database structure. Patient records, personnel files, and inventory lists are often stored as master files.
- **Table files:** Contain data used in calculations. Tax tables and postage rates are often stored as table files.
- **Transaction files:** Used to produce reports and update the master file.
- **Work files:** Temporary files used to make programs run more efficiently.
- **Report files:** Temporarily hold system output.

There are four main organization strategies for files:

- **Linked Lists:** Each record contains a pointer to the next logical record.
- **Hashed Files:** The address of a record can be calculated from the record key.
- **Indexed Lists:** An index to the data file is stored in a separate file.
- **Indexed-Sequential Access Method (ISAM):** Records are stored in order within blocks. An index file is used to access blocks.

Databases can be organized as hierarchical, network, or relational structures.

- **Hierarchical Structures:** All relationships are one-to-one or one-to-many.
- **Network Structures:** Relationships can be many-to-many.
- **Relational Structures:** One or more two-dimensional tables with related attributes.

Designing Data Processing

In the data processing design stage, the analyst determines:

- What algorithms are needed to process the data
- What programming languages should be used
- What specific hardware will be needed
- What manual procedures will be used

Data processing is usually designed top-down. Analysts should consider the relationships, dependencies, and hierarchies within the system.

During the design phase, data processing tasks can be broken down into logical subtasks, or "modules." A modular approach to data processing design often yields a system that is easier to implement, debug, and maintain. Module programs should be a manageable size. Preferably, each module should only have a single function. The design should minimize the number of modules involved in regular maintenance.

Implementation

After the plans for the system have been detailed, the system is built, tested, and installed.

Constructing the System

Before the system can be tested and installed, the components must be gathered. Information systems are built from personnel, hardware, software, stored data, and procedures.

The specific users for the system are defined during the implementation phase. The analyst should keep in mind who will need access to what information. Special training may be needed before cutting over to the new system.

In some cases, the new system is implemented on hardware that exists within the organization. If new hardware is needed, however, the analyst should evaluate alternatives and document the reason for the final choices.

The software needed for the system is developed, purchased, or modified at this stage. Databases or files for the stored data are constructed and populated with sample data until the system can be tested. Procedure manuals are written so future users and analysts will be able to maintain or change the system.

Testing the System

After individual components of the system are tested, the entire system is run with sample data. Outputs are checked with expected results. Any errors are analyzed and corrected. This process continues until no errors are detected.

Installing the System

After all users are trained on the new system procedures, the organization's data is transferred into the new system.

There are several different strategies for switching over from the old system to the new system:

- **Parallel:** Both the old and new system are used for a specific period of time.
- **Phased:** The new system is divided into parts. The parts are introduced individually to allow users to adapt to the system gradually.
- **Plunge:** The old system is retired and the new system is used immediately.
- **Pilot:** Part of the organization uses the new system before it is introduced to the entire organization.

The strategy used depends on how much risk the organization is willing to take and how much money can be used for the transfer process. The plunge method is the most risky but the least expensive. The parallel strategy is the most expensive but offers the most security in the event the new system fails.

Maintenance

There are three reasons maintenance may be required for an information system:

- **Errors are found.** There may be some system errors that escaped the testing process.
- **New functions are needed.** As the organization grows and changes, new outputs or processes may be added.
- **System requirements change.** Tax rates, pay scales, or reporting schedules may need to be adjusted.

Contemporary Approaches

Modern system development strategies can be used instead of or in collaboration with the traditional SDLC.

Prototyping

A prototype of a system includes sample forms, screens and reports so that the user can see what a system will do before the system is constructed. Prototyping helps analysts better understand user requirements.

Rapid Application Development

Rapid application development (RAD) helps shorten system development time by using prototyping and CASE software. RAD techniques often require heavy user involvement in the system development so that the analyst better understands the system requirements and fewer modifications will be needed.

Object-Oriented Analysis and Design

Object-oriented (O-O) analysis and design combines data storage with instructions for processing. O-O methods are often used with the SDLC because:

- They yield constructs that can be reused, often reducing the time and money needed to develop the system.
- Graphical user interfaces (GUIs) may be easier to build and integrate into the system.
- Maintaining software based on O-O programming languages is often simpler than for those built on traditional platforms.
- O-O constructs are often more flexible than their traditional counterparts.

O-O methods are based on six basic ideas: objects, classes, messages, encapsulations, inheritance, and polymorphism.

- **Objects:** An object is any event, item, or person that is represented within the system. For a college course registration system, objects might include students, teachers, courses, start times, departments, and grades.
- **Classes:** Groups of similar objects are represented by classes. If two objects are in the same class, they share a set of attributes. In a college course registration system, all teachers have names, identification numbers, departments, and contact information.
- **Messages:** A message is any information that is sent from one object to another. Teachers, for instance, may send course grades to their departments through the college course registration system.
- **Encapsulation:** Encapsulation is a core idea in O-O methods. Encapsulation means that object records contain directions for changing the object's attributes ("behaviors") as well as the attributes themselves. Encapsulation helps ensure the integrity of the system, as it prevents small changes to individual objects from causing cascading events throughout the system.
- **Inheritance:** In O-O techniques, one class can be derived from another class. The "child class" inherits the attributes and behaviors from the "parent class." The child class may also have additional attributes and behaviors. A class for "Visiting Students"—those who are spending only a semester at the college and then will return to their regular schools—may be derived from the class "Students." "Visiting Student" records would contain all of the types of information from the "Student" class, such a student name, ID number, major, and contact information. In addition, the derived "Visiting Student" class may contain additional attributes such as the student's home school and home contact information.

- **Polymorphism:** Polymorphism means that the same message sent to different classes may have different effects, even if the message relates to the same attribute in each class.

Waterfall

One of the earliest methodologies is the waterfall methodology. With this methodology, a project is entirely completed, from start to finish, working through each of the seven phases in sequence. This methodology is now considered ineffective because often there are changes made midway through a project, or it is simply too time-consuming.

End-User Computing

End-user computing involves the people who will ultimately be using the new system in all stages of system development. The goals of end-user computing approaches include:

- Fewer miscommunications between the users and the analysts
- A finished system that better meets the users' needs
- Better user acceptance of the new system
- Well-trained users who can maintain the system. End-users play different roles throughout the SDLC.

Planning

The end-user may initiate the planning phase by identifying a problem with or a situation not addressed by the current system. The analyst may interview users in order to better understand and define the issues.

Analysis

In the analysis phase, users can help the analyst define the system requirements. Prototypes can help the analyst narrow down what the user really wants from the system.

Design

An end-user approach to design involves the user in choosing the forms, screens, and reports. The analyst may create several mockups and allow end-users to select the ones that they find most attractive and useful.

Implementation

Users may be involved in testing a system to ensure that it is easy to use and provides the necessary output.

Maintenance

Users may notice problems with a new system as time progresses, or see new ways the system can be used. End-users may be trained to do regular maintenance activities, such as update tax rates or prices.

"End-user computing" can also refer to individual information systems, developed by a user in response to a problem. In this case, the SDLC often proceeds informally. For instance, the user may identify a problem (planning phase), investigate how things are currently done as opposed to what needs to be accomplished (analysis phase), decide how to solve the problem by researching software and hardware options (design phase), purchase, install, and begin using the chosen hardware and/or software (implementation phase).

Organization of MIS

There are many positions that may work together within an MIS organization, including:

- **System Analysts/System Administrator:** Analyze information flow within a system in order to suggest improvements or design new systems. Interview users to identify system requirements. Design systems that help users access the information they need. Suggest hardware, software, and policy solutions to business problems. Other responsibilities of a systems administrator include developing the system and watching for potential bugs, routinely checking that the system is operating correctly, backing up the system, updating hardware and software, managing accounts and monitoring access, regulating authorization, and securing the system.
- **Technical Support Specialists:** Provide technical help to end users. Help identify causes and solutions for software, hardware, and system problems. May work for a vendor or within an organization.
- **Information Systems Managers:** Manage system analysts and related team members. May do some system analyst responsibilities, such as analyze data flow and design new information systems. Coordinate the selection, purchase, installation, and maintenance of hardware and software. Suggest solutions to business information problems.

- **Database Administrators (DBAs):** Audit, maintain, update, and develop organizational databases. Archive data and monitor security functions of systems. Design and implement security measures. Make sure database structure is efficient to meet the organization's needs.

- **Network System Administrators:** Analyze organization's network needs. Design LANs, WANs, intranets, and other communication systems to facilitate transfer of information throughout the organization. Respond to security breaches and help design new security measures. Update organization's networks, troubleshoot application, and provide training to end users.

- **Web Designers:** Create websites that promote organization's mission, services, and/or products. Maintain and troubleshoot website.

In addition, the following people may play key roles in the analysis, design, and implementation of an information system:

- **Technical Writers:** Document system analysis, design, implementation, procedures, and policies. Write training materials for end users.

- **Knowledge Workers:** Broadly defined, a knowledge worker is any person who collects or uses knowledge. A more specific explanation is that knowledge workers are people who primarily work with knowledge or information. The collection of information, and knowledge, has been greatly increased with increasing technology. This opens many opportunities involved with understanding it. Knowledge workers are involved in obtaining, analyzing, organizing, and distributing that knowledge (among other things). Knowledge workers can include programmers, students, teachers, experts, analysts, researchers, managers, doctors, and many other professions.

- **Graphic Artists:** Develop attractive and usable input and output forms. Help develop graphical user interfaces (GUIs) and screen layouts. Help design websites for the organization.

- **Ergonomic Specialists:** Design workstations and data input systems that are comfortable and physically safe.

Relationship of MIS to the Enterprise

The average business enterprise has sales, manufacturing, accounting, finance, and personnel functions. Management information systems can support business processes at all levels for functions throughout the organization.

Sales Functions

An MIS may support the sales function of a business at the operational level by processing orders. Expert systems, for example, may be used to determine if inventory is in stock and if certain shipping options are available. At the tactical management level, an MIS can help managers track sales based on categories, geography, and other variables. At the strategic decision level, decision support systems and executive support systems help managers forecast future sales trends.

Manufacturing Functions

MISs help business improve their manufacturing processes at the operational level by helping automate control of material movement. For example, an information system might automatically order parts from the best vendor if the enterprise's stores get low. At the tactical management level, a system might help control inventory by tracking what retail establishments are selling what types of goods, and comparing that information to what is being manufactured. At the strategic decision level, MISs help decision-makers plan future manufacturing operations by tracking current internal and external trends.

Accounting Functions

At the operational level, MISs manage accounts payable and accounts receivable by paying invoices and issuing bills. At the tactical management level, MISs provide the information and support needed to calculate annual budgets. At the strategic decision level, an MIS may be used to forecast future budget needs and expenditures.

Finance Functions

Information systems help enterprises at the operational level by supporting cash management functions such as reconciling accounts and managing short term investments. At the tactical management level, MISs analyze capital investments. At the strategic decision level, information systems help decision makers make long-term investments to maximize the enterprise profit.

Personnel/Human Resource Functions

At the operational level, employee records are often entered, stored, accessed, and updated through an information system. At the tactical management level, knowledge systems may help employees and managers weigh relocation options and strategies. At the decision support level, MIS can help decision makers plan for future personnel needs, including hiring, firing, training, and relocating employees.

 Value of the MIS Function

Each department within an enterprise may have its own information system, but usually it is more beneficial to an organization if the systems are integrated. Information flow in an enterprise may occur:

- Between employees within the same department
- Between employees in different departments
- Between the enterprise and its business partners
- Between the enterprise and its suppliers
- Between the enterprise and its customers

Because of the amount and importance of information flowing into, within, and out of most organizations, it is important that management information systems are able to provide high quality information, in a timely fashion, to the people who need it.

To be of the most value to the enterprise, an information system must provide information that is:

- Accurate
- Concise, without extraneous data
- Consistent with other data in the system
- Available quickly
- Up-to-date
- In the required form

A well-designed information system stocked with high quality information may provide many benefits to an enterprise, including:

- Better employee and department performance
- Lower total information technology cost
- Increased customer satisfaction
- More effective long-term planning
- Cost management through effective comparisons of suppliers and service providers
- Improved communication between enterprise members, regardless of geographic separation

 MIS Administration and Management

Management information system operations within an organization are often divided into three groups: programming/analysis, database administration, and web development.

Programmers and system analysts help design, maintain, and develop systems to support the enterprise goals. Database administrators analyze, maintain, design, and develop database systems to store and process the organization's information. The web development team creates and maintains internet-based systems to facilitate communication within the organization and between the organization and its customers, clients and suppliers.

The programming/analysis, database administration, and web development divisions may all report to a single manager, the Director, or Manager of Management Information Systems. The Director of Management Information Systems is often in charge of:

- Ensuring the programming, database, and internet operations are coordinated
- Making sure all information systems are in compliance with federal, state, local, and industrial security and privacy regulations
- Approving the distribution of resources, including money, human resources, hardware, and software, to information system projects
- Identifying operational issues which can be solved through management information systems
- Approving system designs
- Monitoring system performance and determining when upgrades and changes are required

TELECOMMUNICATIONS

Terminology

Telecommunication is a general term for communicating across a network. This kind of communication requires two types of specialized hardware:

- **Communications channel:** The link between users over which data is transmitted (for example, telephone lines and Ethernet wires).
- **Communication processors:** The link between the computer and the communications channels (for example, modems and Ethernet cards).

Point-to-point communication occurs when users communicate using one communication channel and limited processors. **Network communication** is telecommunication using one or more channels and many communication processors. Point-to-point communication often involves simple communication software while network communication uses more sophisticated applications.

Communication channels can be divided into two sets based on their signal type. **Digital signals** are those that send bits as high and low pulses. **Analog signals** send data in a constantly modulating wave pattern. Telephone lines may be either analog or digital.

Channels can also be described by their maximum **data rates**. Data rate is usually measured in the number of bits transmitted each second ("bits per second," or bps). Saying that a channel has a "low bandwidth" means that it transmits relatively few bits per second.

Channels may use one or a combination of several different media:

- Wire cables
- Fiber-optic cables
- Microwaves
- Radio waves
- Infrared light

Microwaves, radio waves, and infrared light are forms of wireless communication.

Communication processors can also be divided into two main groups. **Channel interface devices** connect directly to a computer. **Communication control units** allow several computer terminals to share a channel. Channel interface devices include modems, cable modems, and terminal adapters. Communication control units include **multiplexers**, which combine several slow devices to make a faster channel, and **controllers**, which make efficient use of the channel by storing signals from each device and releasing them when appropriate.

Protocols are communication rules between computers. Protocols signal when the communication starts and stops as well as what language the transmission will be in (for example, ASCII or Unicode). **Protocol converters** are used to make communication possible between computers that use different protocols.

Specialized software applications are required for telecommunication. If the computer will be linked to a server, **client software** is needed in order to exchange data with the server. Other communication software includes file transfer protocols (ftp), email programs, and web browsers.

Networks

A computer network may involve as few as three computers. The internet is a network of millions of computers and servers. Each computer within a network is called a node.

Networks come in many configurations:

- **Mesh:** Every computer in the network is linked to every other computer.
- **Star:** There is a central computer. Every other computer in the network is linked to the central computer.
- **Hierarchy:** One node is linked to several child nodes. Each of these is the parent to another level of nodes.
- **Bus:** Each computer is linked linearly to a single communication channel ("bus").

SUMMARY OF NETWORK CONFIGURATIONS			
Structure	*Advantage*	*Disadvantage*	*Diagram*
Mesh	Quick and efficient data transmission	Adding new nodes difficult	
Star	Data travels only a short distance	Entire network down if central computer fails	
Hierarchy	More reliable, as network can survive if a lower level node fails	Data must travel longer distance, therefore slower data flow	
Bus	Reliable, network very resilient if any computer fails	Very slow data flow	
Ring	Reliable, as in a bus configuration	Slow	

Network designs work on a continuum of reliability and speed. The most reliable configurations are usually the slowest. Hybrid systems try to maximize the benefits of two or more designs.

Networks may be divided into two general types based on their size. A **local area network (LAN)** covers a small geographic area, like a hospital campus or an office building. **Wide area networks (WANs)** cover large geographic areas, like a city or several countries. **Internetworks** are comprised of connected LANs and WANs.

Local Area Networks

LANs can be wired or wireless. They are usually ring or bus networks and require specialized hardware and software. A network interface card (NIC) connects a computer to the communications channel. Applications are needed to allow the node to send and receive information across the network.

A LAN may include resource servers that can be accessed by the client computers:

- **Print server:** Allows every computer connected to the server to share the printer.
- **File server:** Allows connected computers to share a secondary storage device.
- **Database server:** Server connected to a secondary storage device used in database processing throughout the LAN.

Wide Area Networks and Internetworks

WANs may be star, hierarchical, or hybrid configurations and may include many types of computers. Internetworks are used to connect individual LANs and WANs. Connections between similar networks, such as two LANs, are achieved through a bridge. Two different networks, a LAN and a WAN for instance, are linked with a gateway. A router is used to direct messages to the correct destinations throughout the connected networks.

The internet is a public internetwork which contains a collection of web pages, each identified by a unique uniform resource locator (URL). The internet has become so popular, that many organizations use an intranet, which is a network based on the internet but limited to internal users.

In addition to classifications of networks, there are also many elements within a network that require explanation. Although some networks connect through token ring topology, in which devices are connected in a circle, many topologies connect through hubs. The computers and other devices are all connected directly to the hub, and thereby indirectly connected to each other. Switches perform a similar function as hubs in that they can be used to connect computers in a network. However, they can generate increased productivity because they allow for two-way communication, meaning that messages can be sent and received at the same time. Another advantage over hubs is that switches allow data to be transferred directly between two computers, rather than broadcasted over an entire network.

Routers and firewalls are used to regulate the connections between networks. Routers establish a connection between networks and then regulate the traffic over that connection. One common use of a router is to connect a school or office network to the internet (which is a network itself). The router transmits data between the two, and can deny access where necessary. A firewall is a device which prevents unauthorized access to a network. Because routers can deny access to a network they function as one type of firewall, but the classification includes many additional functions. Firewalls are specifically created to protect a network, and screen all of the data, either sent or received, that passes through it.

Relevance to Business

LANs

LANs can be an effective and efficient way for users throughout an organization to share information and resources. Client/server systems, where data is stored in a centralized database on the server and then sent to client computers as users require it, are often preferred over multiple-user computer systems for many reasons:

- In client/server environments, the server does not handle the data processing, database management, or user interface. This allows the organization to buy a smaller computer to act as a server than would be required for the central computer of a comparable multiple-user system.
- It is cheaper and easier to add new client computers as the company grows than it is to add additional multiple-user computers.

WANs

WANs are often preferred by businesses that have operations separated by long distances. WANs may be based on public or private communication networks. Depending on the size of the area that needs to be connected, businesses may purchase their own cables or wireless system, or they can lease long-distance channels—usually the more economical choice for networks that span very large areas.

Businesses may choose to purchase the hardware and software required to connect to a WAN, or they may contract long-distance links and value-added networks with a communications company. A value-added network (VAN) includes additional software and hardware the company may find useful.

Businesses may choose to use the internet instead of a common carrier channel or VAN. In this case, security measures such as data encryption and user authentication may be needed to protect company information and correspondence.

Electronic Commerce

Organizations often use networks to facilitate electronic commerce (e-commerce). E-commerce involves a web server, which stores the pages of the business's website and is equipped with specialized software. An organization may use its own web server or one provided by an internet service provider (ISP).

A web server is often linked to a database server by a LAN. The database server contains information necessary for e-commerce, for example product availability and prices. A customer initiates an e-commerce transaction by accessing the business's website. When a customer places an order, the web server uses information from the database server to process orders. The order information is sent back to the customer.

Security

Organizations need to keep their information secure while it is being stored ("at rest"), and when it is being transferred across a network ("in motion"). Federal, state, local, and industrial regulations set standards for adequate security. Organizations that are not compliant with these ordinances may face legal sanctions and fines.

Records that should be protected include information about customers, employees, and business processes. In addition, organizations often want to protect their financial records, business processes, marketing strategies, and future plans.

Information security breaches can be the result of either malicious or nonmalicious attacks. Malicious attacks, those that are intended to gain access to or harm secure information, may be the work of hacking, disgruntled employees, organized crime, or espionage. Nonmalicious attacks are often caused by careless employees and poorly-trained system users.

There are five classes of attacks identified by the National Security Agency:

- **Passive attacks** include capturing passwords or other data by monitoring communications.
- **Active attacks** cause corrupted files, denial of service, or information disclosure by overriding security systems or introducing malicious programs.
- **Close-in attacks** require the physical presence of the attacker to access information or to corrupt files.
- **Insider attacks** are those by people within the organization.

- **Distribution attacks** are malicious changes in the system hardware or software during distribution or construction. For example, a programmer may leave a "back door" in an application to allow future access to the system.

Organizations attempt to protect themselves from attacks by using physical, administrative, and technological safeguards.

Physical Security

Most security breaches can be prevented by adequate physical safeguards. Physical security attempts to prevent the theft and loss of hardware and storage media. Some physical security measures include:

- Limited offsite transport of equipment and disks
- Secure disposal of retired equipment
- Monitored use of equipment

Administrative Security

Administrative safeguards include written policies and procedures addressing issues such as:

- What to do if a data breach is suspected
- Security training
- Who may have access to what data
- Current and future protection needs
- Sanctions if security policies are broken by employees

Technological Security

Technological security includes hardware and software used to keep in motion and data at rest safe. These measures may include:

- Password systems
- Two-way handshakes
- Three-way handshakes
- Digital signatures
- Centralized logging
- External authentication

Password systems

Password systems require users to log in before using selected applications or accessing data. An intercepted password, or a password that has been discovered through a brute force method, make the system vulnerable to access by unauthorized users. In a **brute force attack**, malicious attackers attempt to discover a password by trying all possible combinations.

Organizations can make password systems more effective by:

- Requiring each user to have a unique username and related password. This also allows for better tracking of who is accessing what information.
- Requiring passwords to be longer than a certain number of characters and to contain numbers, letters, and symbols. This increases the number of possible passwords, therefore decreasing the likelihood of a brute force attack finding a password.
- Automatically logging users out when the session becomes inactive.
- Randomly assigning passwords or requiring periodic password changes. Users may be relying on the same password for multiple systems. If one password is intercepted, multiple systems may be vulnerable.
- Using encryption whenever passwords are transmitted across the network.

Handshakes

Handshakes are the exchange of information between different elements of a system in order to confirm authorization before accessing and transmitting information.

In a two-way handshake, the equipment or application requesting data sends an electronic code. Another code is sent by the system element from which data is being requested. Before any information is transmitted, both codes are verified. A three-way handshake requires another verified code from the requestor before data can be transmitted.

Digital signatures

Digital signatures authenticate data transfers through the use of mathematical algorithms. The transmitting element in the system signs the data transfer using a secret formula, the "private key." The receiving element verifies that the signature is authentic using an open "public" key. Digital signatures can be used to verify that changes to data files are from authorized users. This can help maintain the integrity of an information system.

Centralized logging

Centralized logging involves the recording of every entry to, access of, and change within a system. Periodic auditing of the logs can reveal unauthorized users and security flaws. Monitoring logs can help detect brute force attacks before they are successful.

External authentication

External authentication relies on a remote service to determine if users should have access to a system. External systems can offer flexibility for the system manager and convenience for the users. Users only have to log in once to access any information they need, and are authorized for, on the server.

INFORMATIONAL SUPPORT

Dimensions of Management Support

Management information systems are used by an organization's management to make more effective decisions. A decision is a choice among several options. Information is used to increase the decision makers' certainty that they made the best choice.

Dimensions of Management Support

Management decisions are made at the operational, tactical, and strategic levels.

Operational decisions are those that affect the organization over the short term. For instance, daily staffing and production decisions are operational decisions made by low-level managers. Operational decisions are short-term, structured decisions made frequently.

Tactical decisions affect the organization for several months. They often involve policy decisions and are made by middle-level managers. Deciding when to release a new product or use a different supplier is a tactical decision. Tactical decisions are intermediate-term, semi-structured decisions made semi-frequently.

Strategic decisions set the organization's policies, goals, and plans. These decisions are made by top-level managers and affect the organization for years. Deciding to develop and introduce a new product is a strategic decision. Strategic decisions are long-term, unstructured decisions made infrequently.

Each level of decision requires different types of information. Operational decisions usually require detailed information internal to the organization. Strategic decisions need more external information in a summarized form. Tactical decisions rely on a combination of internal/external and detailed/summarized information.

Types of Managerial Decisions					
Type	Term	Made by	Structure	Frequency	Example
Operational	Short term	Low-level managers	Very structured	Very frequent	Daily staffing schedules
Tactical	Intermediate term	Middle-level managers	Semi-structured	Semi-frequent	Choosing a supplier
Strategic	Long term	High-level managers	Unstructured	Infrequent	Changing corporate image

System Types

MIS can support operational, tactical, and strategic management decisions, but specialized information systems can provide more specific information than available through database queries and reports.

Decision Support Systems

A decision support system (DSS) analyzes data from the organization's information system. DSSs are mainly used for tactical and strategic decisions, as they provide a deeper analysis of the information than provided by queries and reports. Although management information systems may output basic analyses of some information, DSSs can provide statistical calculations and mathematical modeling to help the manager predict how decisions will affect the organization in the future.

Recall that the four main functions of any information system are input, output, storage, and processing. A DSS uses input from the MIS in addition to a request for analysis from the user. The user often requests a form of analysis or specific model that will be used in the processing function. The output from the DSS is the analysis result, either on paper or on a screen. The results are usually reported as a summary and may include graphs. A DSS usually stores data in a database, either specific to the DSS or shared with other applications. The processing function for a DSS usually involves complex mathematical algorithms.

Executive Support Systems

An executive support system (ESS), or "executive information system (EIS)," provides reports based on information both internal and external to the organization. Because companies gather a vast amount of data that would be difficult to sort through, the purpose of an ESS is to broadly summarize that data in meaningful ways to aid executives in understanding the position of the company. An ESS conglomerates both information that is internal to the company (such as sales and promotional data) and information that is external to the company (such as information about competitors). An ESS is used to make strategic decisions. As these decisions are often unstructured, the output from an ESS needs to be flexible.

The input for an ESS is in the form of requests for reports and analyses. Output is usually displayed on a screen. Because managers may need many levels of detail in order to make strategic decisions, ESS output allows users to "drill down," or find increasingly detailed information. For example, a manager may call up the profit margin for a particular region of the company, then drill down to see the profit margin by office within the region. Reports are produced on demand.

An ESS usually draws information from several databases throughout the organization. ESSs often use processing functions provided by MISs or DSSs.

Expert Systems

An expert system (ES), unlike an ESS, MIS, or DSS, actually advises the decision maker about what choice to make. Expert systems are programmed using human expert knowledge to analyze specific problems. Expert systems have a knowledge base and are programmed with a set of rules that, when given information, will lead them to a specific conclusion or result, making them useful in analytical fields or situations. For example, some of the most common expert systems are used to aid in medical diagnoses, or for interactive games such as chess and checkers. **Artificial intelligence (AI)** is based on techniques used to imitate human intelligence. ESs use AI to help business managers make decisions.

Some expert systems use a series of rules in an **if-then** structure to guide users through its knowledge base. The **inference engine** uses the input received from the user and the rules in the ES knowledge base to draw conclusions.

An expert system might be used instead of a human advisor to help college students choose appropriate courses. Such a system might have the following rules:

> **Rule 1:** If the student has passed MIS 101, then the student may register for MIS 205.

Rule 2: If a student is a sophomore Management Information Systems major, then the student may register for MIS 205.

Rule 3: If the student has received credit for MIS 107, then the student may not register for MIS 205.

If a student tries to register for MIS 205, the ES will analyze input from the student and from the college database to determine whether or not the student will be allowed to register.

The ES input function includes any information entered by the user. The output is the advice from the system. In the example, the output would be the decision whether or not to allow the student to register for MIS 205. The storage function includes storing, maintaining, and accessing the collection of rules used by the ES. The processing function involves the use of the inference engine to apply the rules from the knowledge base to particular situations.

Flowcharts can be used to map the logical processing of an ES. Most flowcharts use standard nomenclature and symbols.

Standard Flowchart Terms and Symbols		
Term	**Definition**	**Symbol**
Input/Output Process	Data being passed through the system	▭
Flow	Shows how the information moves through the system	→
Conditional (or "Decision")	Usually a yes/no question.	◇

The sample rules from the course registration ES are illustrated on the following flowchart.

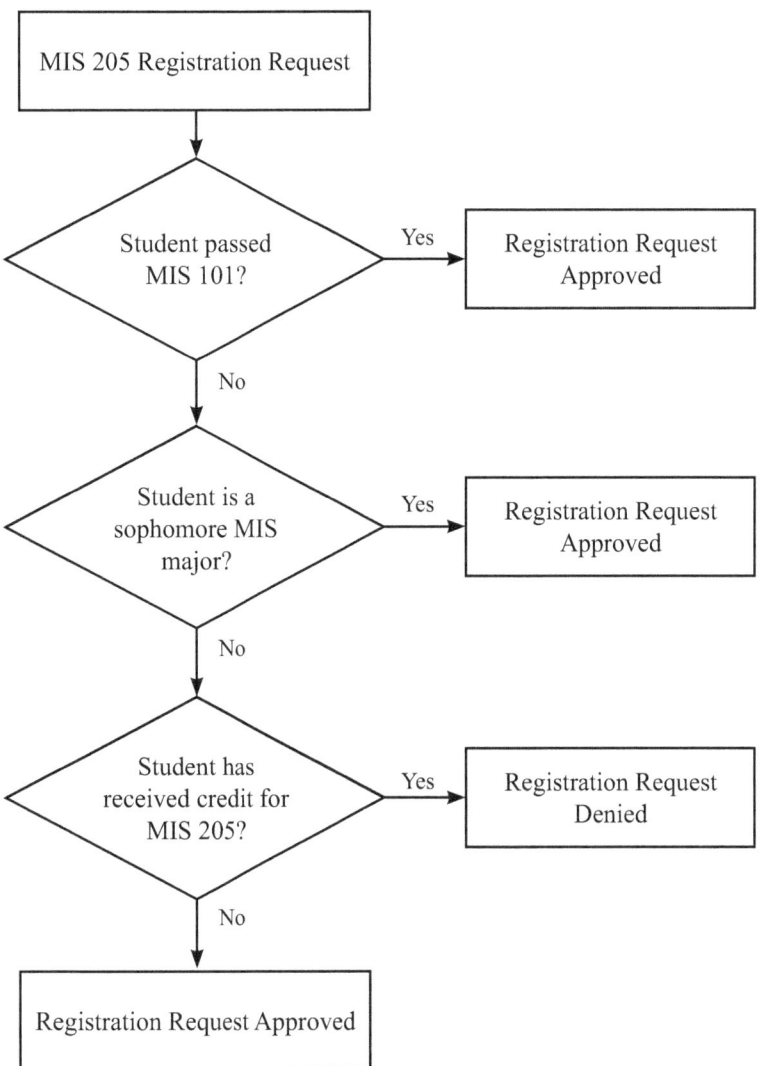

Knowledge Systems

Information refers to data in a meaningful form. **Knowledge** refers to a person's understanding of a situation. Knowledge is gained through intuition, education, experience, and insight. There are two main forms of knowledge:

- **Explicit Knowledge:** Knowledge that can be put in a form that other people can understand. Explicit knowledge can be transmitted to others through verbal or written communication.

- **Implicit Knowledge:** Knowledge that cannot be easily transmitted in verbal or written form.

Organizational knowledge is the whole of the knowledge of everyone in an organization. Like information, knowledge is a resource and should be managed. Knowledge management includes:

- Determining what knowledge exists within the organization
- Documenting what knowledge is needed
- Organizing and recording explicit knowledge in the form of policies, procedures and other documents
- Communicating knowledge within the organization

Knowledge management systems (KMSs), or "knowledge systems," are information systems that help businesses organize, store, and share knowledge. KMSs may include expert systems to help users make decisions using the organizational knowledge. Knowledge systems may also include workgroup applications to facilitate team collaborations.

PROGRAMMING LANGUAGES

Management information systems users may encounter many programming languages, including traditional, object-oriented, and internet-specific languages.

 Traditional Programming Languages

Traditional programming languages are lists of commands that access data stored in the computer system.

- **FORTRAN** ("FORMula TRANslation") was developed by IBM as one of the first third-generation programming languages. FORTRAN is a powerful mathematical language and is often used for scientific and engineering applications.
- **COBOL** ("Common Business Oriented Language") was designed in 1959 to facilitate the creation of business applications.
- **BASIC** ("Beginner's All-purpose Symbolic Instruction Code") was created to help students learn to write programs. Since its release in the 1960s, several versions of BASIC have been released, including the object-oriented Visual Basic.
- **C** was created in the 1970s in an attempt to combine the efficiency of second-generation languages with the convenience and power of third-generation languages. C is used for many operating systems, word processors, and spreadsheet and database applications.
- **Pascal**, also released in the 1970s, attempted to bring more natural language features to programming languages.

 Object-Oriented Programming Languages

Object-oriented languages combine data with their processing instructions to create an "object." Objects can be reused in different programs.

- **C++** is based on the traditional programming language C, but includes object-oriented features.
- **C#** simplifies the syntax used in C++ and adds internet programming functions.
- **Visual FoxPro** is most often used for database management and includes extensive query, report, and form features.

 Programming Languages for the Internet

Some languages have been created specifically for web sites and other internet-based applications.

- **Hypertext Markup Language (HTML)** allows programmers to format text for internet browsers.
- **Extensible Markup Language (XML)** is used to define other languages, letting programmers create detailed ways of describing special forms and documents that are transmitted over the internet.
- **Java** is an object-oriented language based on C. It is used to write applications that can be accessed through an internet browser.

 Examples Code from Common Programming Languages

The traditional way to demonstrate the basic syntax of a programming language is the "Hello World!" example. The "Hello World!" method shows a simple program that will output the phrase "Hello World!" on the computer screen.

Becoming familiar with the "Hello World!" examples of commonly-used programming languages helps users and IS professionals identify languages when they encounter more complex pieces of code. The following table gives the "Hello World!" example code for the languages a user is most likely to encounter.

| Samples for Common Programming Languages ||
Language	Code Sample
FORTRAN	WRITE (6,7) 7 FORMAT(13H Hello World!) STOP END

COBOL	IDENTIFICATION DIVISION.
	   PROGRAM-ID. HELLOWORLD.
	   PROCEDURE DIVISION.
	   PARA-1.
	      DISPLAY "Hello World!"
	      STOP RUN.

BASIC	10 PRINT "Hello World!"
C	```#include <stdio.h>

int main(void)
{
    printf("Hello World!\n");

    return 0;
}``` |
| Pascal | program HelloWorld(output);
begin
   writeln('Hello World!')
end. |
| C++ | ```#include <iostream>
#include <ostream>

int main()
{
    std::cout << "Hello World!" << std::endl;
    return 0;
}``` |

Samples for Common Programming Languages	

C#	class HelloWorldClass
	{
	static void Main()
	   {
	      System.Console.WriteLine("Hello, world!");
	   }
	}

Visual FoxPro	loForm = CREATEOBJECT("HelloWorld") loForm.Show(1)
	
	DEFINE CLASS HiForm AS Form
	   AutoCenter = .T.
	   Caption = "Hello World!"
	
	ADD OBJECT lblHi as Label WITH ;
	   Caption = "Hello World!"
	ENDDEFINE

Java	// HelloWorld.java
	public class HelloWorld {
	public static void main(String[] args) { System.out.println("Hello World!");
	}
	}

HTML	Hello World!
HTML (output in italics)	<i>Hello World!</i>
HTML (output in bold)	<b>Hello World!</b>

ISSUES

The most efficient information systems answer to a business problem is not always the best solution. As technology grows more sophisticated and ubiquitous, serious ethical and security questions are raised.

Ethics

Ethics refers to the rules people use to decide if a behavior is right or wrong. Many organizations have a written code of ethics to help guide decision makers. Some common approaches to ethics include:

- **Utilitarianism:** Making decisions based on what would benefit the most people.
- **Ethical Egoism:** Making decisions based on what is best for the organization.
- **The Golden Rule:** Making decisions based on avoiding harm to others.
- **Categorical Imperative:** Making decisions based on how you would like everyone to make them.

Information systems professionals must consider the ethical considerations of the decisions they make, and organizations must determine what constitutes an ethical use of their information systems and technology. Some ethical issues especially important to information systems include accuracy, use, property, access, and privacy.

Accuracy

Information systems that provide inaccurate outputs can have dangerous consequences, especially in fields such as health care, transportation, and construction design. Systems should complete all of their functions (input, storage, processing, and output) accurately. Inaccurate data at the input function will result in inaccurate data through all the subsequent functions, so safeguards should be in place to verify inputs.

Inaccuracy in the storage and processing functions are called bugs. Managers must decide whether or not it is ethical to release a system with known bugs by weighing the severity of the errors, the time and money required to fix the errors, and the possible consequences of the errors.

Use

The use of information systems can bring up ethical decisions. For example, when a decision support system is used to model future financial changes for a corporation, how much confidence should the organization have in the results before making the findings public—especially if there are implications for the employees, stockholders, and surrounding location?

Property

Recall that information is a resource. Who owns the personal information about someone, the person himself or the organization that has gathered it? What rights does an organization have regarding the information it collects? Should an organization be allowed to sell information about its customers, employees, and suppliers?

Knowledge systems can be particularly problematic with regards to property issues. If an organization bases a decision-making system on the knowledge of its employees, who owns the knowledge—the employees or the organization? Should the organization be able to sell or share the knowledge of its members? How should people be compensated for their knowledge?

Even the pathways over which data is transmitted can raise ethical dilemmas. Who owns wireless signals? What should be allowed on public airwaves? Should it be illegal to intercept data sent over wireless connections?

Access

Information system access can be divided into two categories: physical access and information access.

Physical access involves access to hardware and software. Organizations must address who has access to these resources and for what uses. Should an employee use a corporate computer to play games, or the company's word processing application to write a personal letter?

Information access ethics addresses who should be allowed to view and use what types of information. Should libraries allow access to adult websites when they provide public internet access? If so, should they allow everyone access or just people over a certain age? Should an employee be allowed to use a company's customer email list to publicize a charity event?

Privacy

Who should have access to an individual's contact, financial, personal, and medical information? How much responsibility does an organization have in keeping certain information private?

Federal, state, and local regulations attempt to define privacy ethics with regard to information systems. Some of the most important privacy legislations in the United States include:

- **The Children's Online Privacy Protection Act (COPPA):** Requires certain websites to post privacy policies, describe their information collection policies, and maintain confidentiality of information collected from children.

- **The Fair Credit Reporting Act (FCRA):** Promotes the accuracy and security of records used by credit reporting agencies.

- **The Financial Modernization Act ("Gramm-Leach-Bliley Act," 1999):** Requires financial institutions such as banks, lending services, and tax preparers to take steps to protect customer records.

- **The Computer Matching and Privacy Act (1988):** "Matching" is the process of comparing files in different databases to find out more information about an individual. This act describes how the government can use matching techniques.

- **Electronic Communications Privacy Act (1986):** Details legal ramifications for unauthorized interception of electronically transmitted data.

- **Right to Financial Privacy Act (1978):** Describes how and why the government is allowed to use financial information about individuals.

- **Privacy Act (1974):** Delineates how the government can use information it collects about individuals.

- **Freedom of Information Act (1967):** Allows individuals to inspect the information the government stores about them.

Data Mining

As technology has improved, the ability of corporations to gather information has increased as well. Companies are able to collect and store massive amounts of information that they previously weren't able to. Because of this, it is important that new ways are developed to process and analyze this information. The processes used to analyze data and come to conclusions based on information not given by the raw data alone is referred to as data mining. Some of the types of data mining include cluster analysis, association detection, and statistical analysis. Cluster analysis divides a data set into independent groups, or clusters, that are unique from each other to help offer insights to those analyzing the data. Association detection is used in looking for relevant similarities and commonalities. For example, noting that customers who buy bread are highly likely to buy butter at the same time is a form of association detection. Finally, statistical analysis looks for correlations in other ways, such as time distribution.

Metadata is most simply data about data. Metadata is used to describe the essentials about a piece of data, such as who created it, when they did so, what the data is, what form it is stored in and other such questions. Metadata is essential in organizing and storing information in data warehouses (databases which hold the combined information gathered from a company's internal and external sources).

Security

Information system security involves policies, hardware, and software to help organizations meet the following goals:

- Reduce data theft
- Comply with federal, state, local, or industry standards
- Protect data from unauthorized changes
- Authenticate records and transactions
- Decrease time lost because of data breaches or system issues

Some ordinances that govern information system security include:

- **Gramm-Leach-Bliley Act (GLBA)**, which requires banks and other financial institutions to perform risk analyses of their current security and write a plan for future security plans.
- **Health Insurance Portability and Accountability Act (HIPAA)**, which regulates how certain personal information can be used and released.
- **The California Information Practice Act** requires businesses to notify any employees, clients, or customers in California if there has been a suspected or verified information security breach.

Security breaches can have widespread consequences on an organization, including:

- Sanctions and legal fees if the organization is not using compliant security measures
- Cost of retrieving compromised records
- Loss of customer and employee trust
- Increased information system costs to improve security
- Bad publicity

E-COMMERCE

The buying and selling of goods and services over the internet is referred to as e-commerce. There are four general formats through which e-commerce occurs: Business to Business (B2B), Business to Consumer (B2C), Consumer to Business (C2B), and Consumer to Consumer (C2C). The first form of e-commerce, B2B, includes situations in which businesses interact over the internet. If a grocery store, which is a business, finds and pays for boxes of cereal from a manufacturer, which is also a business, over the internet then it would be an example of B2B e-commerce.

The second form, B2C, is the one that most people would think of. This is when companies sell products over the internet. For example, many large supermarket chains also offer a full array of products which can be purchased online and delivered to customers' homes. Some companies even exist exclusively online. The third form of e-commerce, C2B, occurs when consumers post their payment offers or budgets for goods or services online, and businesses decide whether they are willing to accept at that price. In this way, consumers can make offers to multiple companies at once without having to negotiate with them individually.

 # Sample Test Questions

1) ETL is the acronym describing a data warehousing process. What does the T in ETL stand for?

   A) Translate
   B) Transcript
   C) Transpose
   D) Transform

The correct answer is D:) Transform. ETL stands for extract, transform, load.

2) What does the acronym GIGO stand for?

   A) Garbage in, garbage out
   B) Gigabytes incoming, gigabytes outgoing
   C) Get data in, get data out
   D) Gigabyte internalization and gigabyte optimization

The correct answer is A:) Garbage in, garbage out.

3) Records are grouped together into what kind of structure?

   A) Table
   B) Database
   C) Field
   D) File

The correct answer is D:) File.

4) Moore's law relates to

   A) The amount of available technology
   B) The geographic dispersion of technology
   C) The number of different integrated circuits
   D) Data density

The correct answer is D:) Data density. In other words, the number of transistors per square inch on an integrated circuit.

5) Computer software is a set of

   A) Circuits
   B) Rules
   C) Programs
   D) DBMs

The correct answer is C:) Programs. Most simply put, computer software is a set of programs and algorithms which a computer refers to in order to run.

6) What is the term used to describe data in a useful form?

   A) Fields
   B) Output
   C) Processed
   D) Information

The correct answer is D:) Information.

7) What is information technology?

   A) The processes, people, equipment, policies, and data needed to communicate data
   B) An information system that uses a computer
   C) The computers, fax machines, telephone systems, and other equipment used to facilitate the transfer of information
   D) All of the above

The correct answer is C:) The computers, fax machines, telephone systems, and other equipment used to facilitate the transfer of information.

8) What is another term for an organizational information system?

   A) Operational information system
   B) Corporate information system
   C) Conglomerate information system
   D) Enterprise information system

The correct answer is D:) Enterprise information system.

9) Which of the following would likely be used in an operational information system?

   A) WAN
   B) LAN
   C) Peer-to-peer network
   D) Enterprise network

The correct answer is A:) WAN.

10) Which of the following are not shown in context level data flow diagrams?

   A) Entities
   B) Processes
   C) Storage
   D) Information

The correct answer is C:) Storage.

11) What does the following symbol represent in a context level data flow diagram?

   A) Entity
   B) Process
   C) Storage
   D) Information

The correct answer is A:) Entity.

12) EDI is a way for businesses to share documents. It is

   A) The transfer of data in an agreed document type from one person to another.
   B) The transfer of data in a standardized program from one computer to another.
   C) The transfer of data in an agreed formatting structure from one computer system to another.
   D) The transfer of data in a shared network from one computer to another.

The correct answer is C:) The transfer of data in an agreed structure from one computer system to another. EDI stands for Electronic Data Interchange. It can apply to any business documents.

13) What is the name for a report that is prepared only once?

   A) Exception report
   B) Ad hoc report
   C) Scheduled report
   D) Demand report

The correct answer is B:) Ad hoc report.

14) Which of the following correctly identifies two encoding methods?

   A) ASCII and DSS
   B) Unicode and ASCII
   C) DSS and GDSS
   D) GDSS and Unicode

The correct answer is B:) Unicode and ASCII. ASCII (short for American Standard Code for Information Interchange) and Unicode (which was developed by the Unicode Consortium) are both encoding methods.

15) The equation $f(x+1) = f(x) + 2$ is an example of what kind of function?

   A) Recursive
   B) Reflexive
   C) Additive
   D) Communicative

The correct answer is A:) Recursive.

16) Which of the following is true about operations management?

   A) Operations management includes intermediate-term tactics and resource allocation.
   B) Operations management involves allocating resources to develop computer applications for business operations.
   C) Operations management includes workforce scheduling and the routine ordering of supplies.
   D) Operations management is the top layer of management in an organization.

The correct answer is C:) Operations management includes workforce scheduling and the routine ordering of supplies.

17) Which of the following is NOT true about systems?

   A) Systems function through interrelated subsystems.
   B) Systems are not bounded.
   C) Systems can be controlled.
   D) Systems are made of interdependent elements.

The correct answer is B:) Systems are not bounded.

18) Which of the following would NOT be the duty of the database administrator?

   A) Developing the database
   B) Monitoring network activity
   C) Ensuring database security
   D) Maintaining the database

The correct answer is B:) Monitoring network activity. The database administrator is responsible for the database, not the network.

19) Which statement is true about the following diagram?

   A) It is a level 0 data flow diagram.
   B) It is a child diagram.
   C) It is an environmental model.
   D) It is an E-R diagram.

The correct answer is C:) It is an environmental model.

20) Which statement is NOT true about level 0 data flow diagrams?

   A) Data stores connect to external entities.
   B) No more than nine processes should be shown.
   C) They must have the same inputs and outputs as the context level diagram.
   D) The same data should not flow into and out of a single process.

The correct answer is A:) Data stores connect to external entities.

21) Why should an information system analyst study an organization's physical data flow diagrams as well as the logical data flow diagrams?

    A) Physical models distinguish between automated and manual processes.
    B) Most system users find it easier to understand physical data flow diagrams than logical data flow diagrams.
    C) Physical system elements change less frequently than business operations, making it easier to update systems built on the physical model.
    D) The analyst can more easily identify business operations goals using the physical data flow diagram.

The correct answer is A:) Physical models distinguish between automated and manual processes.

22) Who invented the first programmable calculating machine in 1835?

    A) Wilhelm Schickard
    B) Charles Babbage
    C) Basile Bouchon
    D) Jean-Baptist Falcon

The correct answer is B:) Charles Babbage.

23) Normalization is meant to

    A) Reduce redundancy
    B) Increase information capacity
    C) Ensure that only relevant information is stored on tables
    D) Both A and C

The correct answer is D:) Both A and C. Normalization increases efficiency, clarity, and usefulness of databases.

24) Which of the following is NOT true about cathode ray tube (CRT) monitors?

    A) They are less expensive than comparably sized liquid crystal display (LCD) monitors.
    B) They are harder to read in direct sunlight than LCD monitors.
    C) They have a larger footprint than comparably sized LCD monitors.
    D) They are heavier than comparably sized LCD monitors.

The correct answer is B:) They are harder to read in direct sunlight than LCD monitors.

25) Which of the following is NOT a class of printers?

   A) Serial printers
   B) Line printers
   C) Page printers
   D) Parallel printers

The correct answer is D:) Parallel printers.

26) Which of the following is a primary storage device?

   A) Optical disk
   B) Magnetic tape
   C) Silicon chip
   D) Flash drive

The correct answer is C:) Silicon chip.

27) What is a hardware component of the central processing unit (CPU)?

   A) The processing unit
   B) The supervisor
   C) The logical control center
   D) The arithmetic-logic unit

The correct answer is D:) The arithmetic-logic unit.

28) Which group of programming languages is machine-dependent?

   A) Second generation
   B) Third generation
   C) Fourth generation
   D) Fifth generation

The correct answer is A:) Second generation.

29) What are the two types of third generation languages?

   A) Visual and standard
   B) Object-oriented and traditional
   C) Object-oriented and text-based
   D) Visual and web 2.0

The correct answer is B:) Object-oriented and traditional.

30) Metadata is

   A) A complex algorithm used in data storage
   B) Any data referenced in a data warehouse
   C) Data about data
   D) Stored in a data warehouse

The correct answer is C:) Data about data. Metadata is used to describe the essentials about a piece of data, such as who created it, when they did so, what form it is stored in, and other such questions.

31) Which programming language translation method translates individual instructions into machine code, allowing the computer to execute an instruction without translating the entire program?

   A) Interpreter
   B) Compiler
   C) Transducer
   D) Auditor

The correct answer is A:) Interpreter.

32) What is "virtual memory?"

   A) The data files on external storage media
   B) A measure of a system's processing speed under optimal conditions
   C) The ability to run a large program by only loading selected parts into primary memory
   D) Secondary storage files based on the internet or the organization's intranet

The correct answer is C:) The ability to run a large program by only loading selected parts into primary memory.

33) What is meant by "interactivity" in reference to an operating system?

   A) The ability of two or more members of a workgroup to work together on a single file
   B) The ability to run more than one program at the same time, even if both programs access the same data
   C) The ability to access help files to troubleshoot an application while continuing to use the application
   D) The ability to process data as it is inputted

The correct answer is D:) The ability to process data as it is inputted.

34) What is a site map?

   A) A model of the functionality of a system
   B) A diagram of the hierarchy of a system
   C) A content matrix of the system
   D) All of the above

The correct answer is B:) A diagram of the hierarchy of a system.

35) Designing the details of individual entities first is called what?

   A) Top-down architecture
   B) Bottom-up architecture
   C) Detailed content design
   D) User need functionality

The correct answer is B:) Bottom-up architecture.

36) Which of the following is NOT a category of information systems?

   A) Workgroup
   B) Individual
   C) Intraorganizational
   D) Interorganizational

The correct answer is C:) Intraorganizational.

37) What is the general term for collaborative software used with networked computers?

   A) Groupware
   B) Workgroup applications
   C) Telecommunications
   D) Document communications

The correct answer is A:) Groupware.

38) Which of the following is a type of network topology?

   A) LAN
   B) WAN
   C) Token ring
   D) Firewall

The correct answer is C:) Token ring. A topology is the way that a network is arranged. Token rings describe networks that are connected in a circle, with a token that circulates through the network.

39) Which of the following statements is TRUE?

   A) In a token ring topology, all computers are connected to a central hub.
   B) In token rings, all of the computers are connected in a large circle.
   C) Token ring topology is typically used to connect multiple WANs.
   D) Token ring topology is beneficial because it allows all computers to communicate simultaneously.

The correct answer is B:) In token rings, all of the computers are connected in a large circle. A token then passes through the network allowing the transmission of data.

40) What is "electronic conferencing?"

   A) A combination of videoconferencing and whiteboard conferencing
   B) Meetings between group members who are in the same room at the same time, but in separate workspaces where they can key in comments on a common document
   C) Conferencing through a computer network
   D) Viewing the same document at different locations

The correct answer is A:) A combination of videoconferencing and whiteboard conferencing.

41) Which would not be a typical accuracy control used in a transaction processing system (TPS)?

  A) Control totals
  B) Security systems
  C) Audit trails
  D) Backup procedures

The correct answer is B:) Security systems.

42) Which of the following is NOT an example of metadata?

  A) The .doc on the end of a file name used to describe the type of file.
  B) A summary of the information found on a webpage.
  C) A description of the size and designer of an image on a webpage.
  D) A spreadsheet which contains a record of a company's sales.

The correct answer is D:) A spreadsheet which contains a record of a company's sales. This would be data, not metadata.

43) A device which is created to protect a network against unauthorized access is a

  A) Router
  B) Hub
  C) Switch
  D) Firewall

The correct answer is D:) Firewall. Routers are one type of firewall, but there is much more involved in protecting a network as well.

44) Which of the following best describes the role of the sponsor in an interorganizational information system (IOS)?

  A) Establishes and maintains the system
  B) Supplies all the hardware to the system
  C) Provides the telecommunications protocols to the system
  D) Recruits participants to the system

The correct answer is A:) Establishes and maintains the system.

45) What is the name for the technique of allocating each user a small amount of time for processing data before going on to the next user?

   A) Multiple-user
   B) Interactivity
   C) Virtual memory
   D) Time-sharing

The correct answer is D:) Time-sharing.

46) Which of the following is used to help organize and analyze the information in a database?

   A) DSS
   B) EIS
   C) DBMS
   D) ASCII

The correct answer is C:) DBMS. This stands for database management system.

47) The way that relational databases organize information can be compared to a

   A) String
   B) Tree
   C) Line
   D) Web

The correct answer is D:) Web. Hierarchal database models can be compared to a tree.

48) Normalization reduces inefficiency in

   A) Executive information systems
   B) Relational databases
   C) Decision support systems
   D) Management information networks

The correct answer is B:) Relational databases. Because relational databases are designed like a web, redundancy can hinder efficiency.

49) Which is NOT a benefit of using an electronic data interchange (EDI) system?

   A) Data can be transmitted faster through an EDI than by using paper-based methods
   B) Reduced costs over paper-based methods
   C) EDIs are standardized, allowing all organizations to participate
   D) An EDI can transmit data more accurately than a paper-based system

The correct answer is C:) EDIs are standardized, allowing all organizations to participate.

50) John von Neumann is known for creating the first computer model which had

   A) ROM
   B) DSS
   C) Hard drives
   D) Working memory

The correct answer is D:) Working memory. Working memory is now referred to as RAM, and Von Neumann's architecture is still used today.

51) Which of the following is NOT an element of the Von Neumann architecture?

   A) Router
   B) Permanent memory
   C) Working memory
   D) Input

The correct answer is A:) Router. The five elements in the Von Neumann architecture are CPU, input, output, working memory, and permanent memory.

52) Which element is NOT found on an entity-relationship (E-R) diagram?

   A) Entities
   B) Relationships
   C) Data flow
   D) Identifiers

The correct answer is C:) Data flow.

53) On an E-R diagram, what is the name for a specific entity within an entity class?

   A) Particular
   B) Identifier
   C) Unit
   D) Instance

The correct answer is D:) Instance.

54) A device which connects networks and regulates traffic over that connection is a

   A) Router
   B) Hub
   C) Switch
   D) Firewall

The correct answer is A:) Router. One common use of a router is to connect a school or office network to the internet (which is a network itself). The router transmits data between the two, and can deny access where necessary.

55) When two or more computers are linked together to allow communication, exchange of data, and sharing of resources, it is called a

   A) Local Area Network
   B) Metropolitan Area Network
   C) Network
   D) Wide Area Network

The correct answer is C:) Network. The above is the definition of a network. LANs and WANs are specific types of networks.

56) Which of the following statements is FALSE?

   A) WANs are typically more difficult to maintain than LANs.
   B) LANs are used to cover a relatively small geographic spread.
   C) WANs can be composed of a number of LANs.
   D) A WAN would typically be used to connect all the computers in a room.

The correct answer is D:) A WAN would typically be used to connect all the computers in a room. A WAN is used in situations where there is a large geographic spread, not in a single room.

57) Which of the following describes an expert system?

   A) Programs and technology used to replace individuals in low skill jobs.
   B) Programs which are used by experts in their fields to come to innovative and new conclusions.
   C) Software which is designed to simulate the decision-making process.
   D) Applications which help organizations gather information from their top employees.

The correct answer is C:) Software which is designed to simulate the decision-making process. Expert systems are a type of artificial intelligence software which follow a set of rules to reach a conclusion.

58) In the E-R model, relationships of degree 2 are called what?

   A) Binary
   B) Duplex
   C) Coupled
   D) Normalized

The correct answer is A:) Binary.

59) In the E-R model, what are relationships between entire entity classes called?

   A) Full relationships
   B) Relationship classes
   C) Normalized relationships
   D) Coupled relationships

The correct answer is B:) Relationship classes.

60) What is the size, color, and price of an object in the SHIRT entity class called?

   A) Identifiers
   B) Descriptors
   C) Attributes
   D) Characteristics

The correct answer is C:) Attributes.

61) If a specific entity can only be identified using two or more attributes, the identifier is called what?

   A) Compound identifier
   B) Complex identifier
   C) Composite identifier
   D) Multiple identifier

The correct answer is C:) Composite identifier.

62) Which of the following is a type of relationship on an E-R diagram?

   A) 1:1
   B) 1:N
   C) N:M
   D) All of the above

The correct answer is D:) All of the above.

63) On an E-R diagram, what is the term used to describe the maximum number of entity instances involved on each side of a relationship?

   A) Cardinality
   B) Normality
   C) Maximum cardinality
   D) Maximum normality

The correct answer is C:) Maximum cardinality.

64) Data mining is

   A) The process used to sort and analyze data to collect information not reflected by the raw data alone.
   B) An effective way of increasing communication and effectiveness in a work place.
   C) A process of using the internet to discover information not included in a company's raw data.
   D) The buying and selling of goods and services over the internet.

The correct answer is A:) The process used to sort and analyze data to collect information not reflected in the raw data alone. Companies are able to collect and store massive amounts of information that they previously weren't able to.

65) When a company moves a portion of its business to an external location (often international) it is referred to as

   A) Expansion
   B) Globalization
   C) Outsourcing
   D) Insourcing

The correct answer is C:) Outsourcing. Outsourcing is when a company moves part of their business to another location (generally the term is used to describe outsourcing to outside the country which they are located in).

66) How many bits are in a byte of data?

   A) 2
   B) 8
   C) 10
   D) 15

The correct answer is B:) 8.

67) Moore's law states that the number of transistors per square inch will double every

   A) 6 months
   B) 1 year
   C) 18 months
   D) 2 years

The correct answer is C:) 18 months. The original trend was that it doubled each year, however over time it has been amended to 18 months as the speed has slowed.

68) On the E-R diagram below, which element is an attribute?

   A) A
   B) B
   C) C
   D) D

The correct answer is A:) A.

69) On the E-R diagram in number 46, which element displays the maximum number of relationships between each entity class?

   A) A
   B) B
   C) C
   D) D

The correct answer is C:) C.

70) On the E-R diagram in number 46, which element is an entity?

   A) A
   B) B
   C) C
   D) D

The correct answer is B:) B.

71) What is the main difference between entities in the E-R model and semantic objects in the semantic object model?

   A) Semantic objects have attributes that describe relationships.
   B) Semantic objects are not grouped into classes.
   C) Entities do not represent identifiable things.
   D) Entities are only used when describing databases.

The correct answer is A:) Semantic objects have attributes that describe relationships.

72) Which is a true statement about relations in the relational model?

   A) The rows of the relation are called attributes.
   B) They are three-dimensional tables.
   C) The order of the attributes is significant.
   D) The rows of the relation are called tuples.

The correct answer is D:) The rows of the relation are called tuples.

73) The process of breaking down relations to make more efficient structures is called what?

   A) Simplification
   B) Deconstruction
   C) Normalization
   D) Relation optimization

The correct answer is C:) Normalization.

74) What is another term for a data hierarchy?

   A) Architecture
   B) Entity-relationship model
   C) Node
   D) Tree

The correct answer is D:) Tree.

75) What is the name for a single element in a data hierarchy?

   A) Entity
   B) Branch
   C) Node
   D) Child

The correct answer is C:) Node.

76) In the following data hierarchy diagram, what is the term used to describe the relationship between nodes 2, 3, and 4?

   A) Siblings
   B) There is no relationship between nodes 2, 3, and 4
   C) One-to-many
   D) Bifurcation

The correct answer is A:) Siblings.

77) On the diagram from number 54, what term describes node 1?

A) Ancestor
B) Root
C) Propagate
D) Stem

The correct answer is B:) Root.

78) Which of the following most correctly states the purpose of an EIS?

A) To organize data in meaningful ways and aid executives in better understanding an organization.
B) To facilitate basic transactions and record transactional information.
C) To collect and distribute the knowledge available in an organization.
D) To create models that help management in situations where they are unsure of future outcomes.

The correct answer is A:) To organize data in meaningful ways and aid executives in better understanding an organization. Because companies gather a vast amount of data that would be difficult to sort through, the purpose of an ESS is to broadly summarize that data in meaningful ways aid executives in understanding the position of the company.

79) Which of the following is NOT one of the five phases of the SDLC?

A) Design
B) Maintenance
C) Setup
D) Development

The correct answer is C:) Setup. The five phases are planning, analysis, design, implementation, and maintenance.

80) Which of the following is true about data hierarchies?

A) The relationships can be one-to-one, one-to-many, or many-to-many.
B) Child nodes inherit attributes from the parent node.
C) A node may not share attributes with its siblings.
D) The top node of the tree is called the stem.

The correct answer is B:) Child nodes inherit attributes from the parent node.

81) The individual responsible for maintaining and securing a company's network is the

   A) Database administrator
   B) Network manager
   C) Executive system analyst
   D) System administrator

The correct answer is D:) System administrator. The system administrator develops, maintains, and secures the system (or network).

82) E-commerce is

   A) The buying and selling of goods and services over the internet.
   B) Conducting of business over the internet.
   C) The term used to describe online auction sites.
   D) An important type of database management system.

The correct answer is A:) The buying and selling of goods and services over the internet. E-commerce can consist of multiple different combinations of interactions between businesses and consumers.

83) A program which gives a medical diagnosis when a list of symptoms are input is a(n)

   A) Decision Support System
   B) Expert System
   C) Management Information System
   D) Diagnostic Transistor

The correct answer is B:) Expert System. Expert systems are programmed to simulate the decision-making process of experts, primarily in analytical fields.

84) Software which is made freely available, but which cannot legally be altered is

   A) Freeware
   B) Shareware
   C) Groupware
   D) Teamware

The correct answer is B:) Shareware. Shareware is copyrighted but can be downloaded for free. Freeware can be downloaded and used without restriction.

85) Queries are programmed using what language?

   A) Any third-generation programming language
   B) BASIC
   C) SQL
   D) Query generator

The correct answer is C:) SQL.

86) Which of the following is NOT a standard SQL command?

   A) QUERY
   B) INSERT
   C) DELETE
   D) UPDATE

The correct answer is A:) QUERY.

87) Which of the following is NOT required for an individual system to communicate across a network?

   A) Communications channel
   B) Communication processors
   C) Communication control units
   D) All of the above are needed to communicate across a network

The correct answer is C:) Communication control units.

88) Which of the following is a type of communication control unit that combines many slow devices in order to make a faster channel?

   A) Multiplexers
   B) Controllers
   C) Converters
   D) Transformers

The correct answer is A:) Multiplexers.

89) What term is used for devices that enable communication between computers using different protocols?

   A) Transmission converters
   B) Protocol converters
   C) Transmission controls
   D) Translators

The correct answer is B:) Protocol converters.

90) Which of the following would NOT be the responsibility of the system administrator?

   A) Updating and maintaining hardware.
   B) Updating and maintaining software.
   C) Developing a network and ensuring it operates correctly.
   D) Developing and updating databases.

The correct answer is D:) Developing and updating databases. This would be the job of the database administrator, not the system administrator.

91) Which of the following correctly identifies a difference between ASCII and Unicode?

   A) Unicode uses 8-, 16-, or 32-bit characters so it takes up more space than ASCII which uses 7-bit.
   B) ASCII has a much larger character base than does Unicode.
   C) Unicode is most accurate and useful for text in American English.
   D) Both B and C

The correct answer is A:) Unicode uses 8-, 16-, or 32-bit characters so it takes up more space than ASCII which uses 7-bit. ASCII is most commonly used for American English and has a smaller character base.

92) Which of the following e-commerce models describes when consumers post offers for goods or services online and business decide whether they wish to sell at the specified price?

   A) C2C
   B) B2C
   C) C2B
   D) B2B

The correct answer is C:) C2B. C2B is also called consumer to business model.

93) What term describes a networked computer?

   A) Entity
   B) Branch
   C) Node
   D) Child

The correct answer is C:) Node.

94) Which of the following is the best definition for a mesh configuration?

   A) Each computer in the network is linked to every other computer.
   B) There is a central computer, to which every other computer is linked.
   C) One computer is linked to several other computers. Each of these is linked to another level of computers.
   D) The computers are linked circularly to a single communication channel.

The correct answer is A:) Each computer in the network is linked to every other computer.

95) Which of the following is true about a star network configuration?

   A) It is one of the most reliable configurations, as the network can survive if any one computer fails.
   B) Adding new nodes is difficult.
   C) The entire network will fail if the central computer is down.
   D) The nodes are arranged in a circular, central hub.

The correct answer is C:) The entire network will fail if the central computer is down.

96) Which configuration is most likely to be used in a local area network (LAN)?

   A) Ring
   B) Star
   C) Mesh
   D) Hybrid

The correct answer is A:) Ring.

97) What connection is used to join two LANs?

   A) Bridge
   B) Gateway
   C) Router
   D) Hub

The correct answer is A:) Bridge.

98) What connection is used to join a LAN to a WAN?

   A) Bridge
   B) Gateway
   C) Router
   D) Hub

The correct answer is B:) Gateway.

99) What connection is used to direct messages through connected networks?

   A) Bridge
   B) Gateway
   C) Router
   D) Hub

The correct answer is C:) Router.

100) Which statement is most true about a client/server system?

   A) It is the most common WAN system.
   B) It is more expensive to add to than a multiple-user system.
   C) The server handles all data processing and database management.
   D) Data is stored in a centralized database on the server.

The correct answer is D:) Data is stored in a centralized database on the server.

101) Information system attacks are divided into what two types?

   A) Compliant and noncompliant
   B) Internal and external
   C) Foreign and domestic
   D) Malicious and nonmalicious

The correct answer is D:) Malicious and nonmalicious.

102) Which of the following is NOT a class of system attack?

   A) Passive
   B) Distribution
   C) External
   D) Active

The correct answer is C:) External.

103) Security training and written security policies are what type of security?

   A) Physical
   B) External
   C) Technological
   D) Procedural

The correct answer is D:) Procedural.

104) What class of attacks includes capturing passwords by monitoring email transmissions?

   A) Active
   B) Insider
   C) Close-in
   D) Passive

The correct answer is D:) Passive.

105) An attacker tries to figure out a system password by trying all possible combinations. What is this called?

   A) Trial-and-error attack
   B) Logical attack
   C) Distribution attack
   D) Brute force attack

The correct answer is D:) Brute force attack.

106) Which of the following is designed to aid managers in making decisions by creating summary reports?

　　A) Executive Information Systems
　　B) Decision Support Systems
　　C) Transaction Processing Systems
　　D) Management Information Systems

The correct answer is D:) Management Information Systems. A DSS builds on the information in an MIS and also aids in making decisions, but an MIS specifically makes managerial reports.

107) In which phase of the software development lifecycle would it be necessary to determine the feasibility of a project?

　　A) Planning
　　B) Analysis
　　C) Development
　　D) Implementation

The correct answer is A:) Planning. This is the first phase of the SDLC and also involves choosing a development method and project.

108) A person who collects or uses knowledge is a

　　A) Database administrator
　　B) System administrator
　　C) Knowledge management administrator
　　D) Knowledge worker

The correct answer is D:) Knowledge worker.

109) What term described the exchange of information between computers in order to confirm authorization?

　　A) External authentication
　　B) Password system
　　C) Digital signature
　　D) Handshake

The correct answer is D:) Handshake.

110) In a digital signature, what is used by the receiving element?

A) Public key
B) Private key
C) Password
D) External authentication

The correct answer is A:) Public key.

111) Monitoring centralized logs is most effective at detecting what kind of attack?

A) Brute force
B) Passive
C) Trial-and-error
D) Close-in

The correct answer is A:) Brute force.

112) The traditional systems development life cycle (SDLC) proceeds in what order?

A) Analysis, planning, design, implementation, maintenance
B) Planning, analysis, design, implementation, maintenance
C) Planning, design, analysis, implementation, maintenance
D) Planning, design, implementation, analysis, maintenance

The correct answer is B:) Planning, analysis, design, implementation, maintenance.

113) Which of the following would be classified as a knowledge worker?

A) Programmer
B) Student
C) Analysts
D) All of the above

The correct answer is D:) All of the above. Knowledge workers are people involved in collecting, storing, analyzing, using, and distributing knowledge, as all of the examples are.

114) Which person in an organization is responsible to maintain and protect the database?

    A) Executive manager
    B) Database administrator
    C) Executive information officer
    D) Executive technology officer

The correct answer is B:) Database administrator. This position can include developing and improving the database as well as finding ways to making it more effective.

115) A feasibility analysis is conducted in which part of the SDLC?

    A) Design
    B) Analysis
    C) Planning
    D) Implementation

The correct answer is C:) Planning.

116) Which is NOT a goal of the design phase of the SDLC?

    A) Determine how outputted information will be formatted.
    B) Determine what types of data stores will be used in the system.
    C) Determine who will have access to outputted information.
    D) Determine if the system will be created on custom or packaged software.

The correct answer is D:) Determine if the system will be created on custom or packaged software.

117) In which kind of file does each record point to the next logical record?

    A) Linked list
    B) Hashed files
    C) Indexed list
    D) ISAM list

The correct answer is A:) Linked list.

118) Which is NOT a database organization?

   A) Hierarchical
   B) Sequential
   C) Network
   D) Relational

The correct answer is B:) Sequential.

119) Which type of database contains only one-to-one or one-to-many relationships?

   A) Hierarchical
   B) Sequential
   C) Network
   D) Relational

The correct answer is A:) Hierarchical.

120) Which switchover strategy is the least risky?

   A) Parallel
   B) Phased
   C) Plunge
   D) Pilot

The correct answer is A:) Parallel.

121) Which contemporary development strategy uses prototyping, CASE software, and heavy user involvement?

   A) Object-oriented analysis design
   B) End-user design
   C) Rapid application development (RAD)
   D) Collaborative analysis and design

The correct answer is C:) Rapid application development (RAD).

122) Which is NOT a benefit of object-oriented (O-O) analysis and design?

   A) The objects constructed can often be reused in other applications.
   B) Maintaining O-O systems is often easier than those built on traditional platforms.
   C) O-O analysis and design techniques allow the analyst to better understand and plan for user needs.
   D) Graphical user interfaces are easier to build and integrate using O-O languages.

The correct answer is C:) O-O analysis and design techniques allow the analyst to better understand and plan for user needs.

123) Management information systems can be used to support which level of a business's sales functions?

   A) The operational level
   B) The tactical level
   C) The strategic level
   D) All management levels

The correct answer is D:) All management levels.

124) Which of the following is NOT a type of computer software?

   A) Operating systems
   B) Transistors
   C) Computer games
   D) Media players

The correct answer is B:) Transistors. Transistors are a part of the hardware of a computer, not the software.

125) What name is given to programs which allow people to work together to achieve a common goal?

   A) Groupware
   B) Shareware
   C) Malware
   D) Software

The correct answer is A:) Groupware. Groupware is an effective way of increasing communication and effectiveness in a workplace.

126) The electronic exchange of business documents is referred to as

   A) Electronic Data Interchange (EDI)
   B) Executive Data Management Systems
   C) Structured Communication and Data Exchange
   D) Electronic Document Exchange

The correct answer is A:) Electronic Data Interchange (EDI).

127) Which of the following is NOT an example of EDI?

   A) Electronic invoices
   B) Electronic receipts
   C) Electronic shipping notices
   D) Email

The correct answer is D:) Email.

128) Which term describes unstructured decisions that affect an organization over the long term?

   A) Operational
   B) Tactical
   C) Strategic
   D) Mid-level

The correct answer is C:) Strategic.

129) Which type of management information system performs advanced mathematical analyses of organizational data?

   A) Decision support systems (DSSs)
   B) Executive support systems (ESSs)
   C) Expert systems (ESs)
   D) Knowledge systems

The correct answer is A:) Decision support systems (DSSs).

130) Which type of management information system may use artificial intelligence to help managers make decisions?

    A) Decision support systems (DSSs)
    B) Executive support systems (ESSs)
    C) Expert systems (ESs)
    D) Knowledge management systems (KMSs)

The correct answer is C:) Expert systems (ESs).

131) Which of the following correctly identifies the three classifications of groupware?

    A) Communication, collaboration, decision support
    B) Conferencing, data mining, collaboration
    C) Decision support, collaboration, data mining
    D) Communication, collaboration, conferencing

The correct answer is D:) Communication, collaboration, conferencing. The three classifications cover software which is used in basic conversation and information exchange, to those which allow employees to work together on projects.

132) Which of the following is NOT a form of data mining?

    A) Cluster analysis
    B) Association detection
    C) Statistical analysis
    D) Von Neumann algorithm

The correct answer is D:) Von Neumann algorithm. The Von Neumann architecture is a computer model which uses RAM as working memory.

133) Sorting data into unique and independent groups to offer insights about a data set is

    A) Independent analysis
    B) Statistical analysis
    C) Association detection
    D) Cluster analysis

The correct answer is D:) Cluster analysis. Cluster analysis divides a data set into independent groups, or clusters, that are unique from each other to help offer insights to those analyzing the data.

134) On a flowchart, what symbol is used to represent a decision?

   A) Rectangle
   B) Arrow
   C) Diamond
   D) Circle

The correct answer is C:) Diamond.

135) Which ethical approach makes decisions based on what would benefit the most people?

   A) Utilitarianism
   B) Ethical egoism
   C) The golden rule
   D) Categorical imperative

The correct answer is A:) Utilitarianism.

136) Which statute requires banks to analyze their current security?

   A) The California Information Practice Act
   B) Health Insurance Portability and Accountability Act
   C) The Fair Credit Reporting Act
   D) The Gramm-Leach-Bliley Act

The correct answer is D:) The Gramm-Leach-Bliley Act.

137) Which programming language is best suited for most business applications?

   A) FORTRAN
   B) COBOL
   C) BASIC
   D) C

The correct answer is B:) COBOL.

138) Which of these is an object-oriented programming language?

   A) FORTRAN
   B) C-Sharp
   C) BASIC
   D) Pascal

The correct answer is B:) C-Sharp.

139) Which programming language is the following most likely a sample of?

   10 INPUT NAME$;
   20 PRINT "Hello, " NAME$;

   A) FORTRAN
   B) C-Sharp
   C) BASIC
   D) Pascal

The correct answer is C:) BASIC.

140) What is the name of the program that runs the entire time a computer is on?

   A) The processing unit
   B) The supervisor
   C) The logical control program
   D) The arithmetic-logic unit

The correct answer is B:) The supervisor.

141) What is the main difference between a bus network and a ring network?

   A) A bus network is linear. A ring network is a loop.
   B) A bus network connects all nodes to a central bus. A ring network connects the nodes directly to each other.
   C) A bus network is more reliable than a ring network.
   D) A bus network is connected to a central computer ("server"). A ring network is a peer-to-peer network.

The correct answer is A:) A bus network is linear. A ring network is a loop.

142) What is the name for a hardware and software system used to keep unauthorized users from accessing an intranet?

A) A password system
B) A firewall
C) A handshake
D) An external validation

The correct answer is B:) A firewall.

143) Which is NOT an advantage of database processing over file processing?

A) Database processing is less expensive than file processing.
B) There is less duplication of data in a database system.
C) Programs in a database-based system are not dependent on how the database is organized.
D) It is easier to process groups of data in a database system.

The correct answer is A:) Database processing is less expensive than file processing.

144) What are the basic functions of an information system?

A) Word processing, communications, and storage
B) Input, processing, storage, and output
C) Decision making, security, filing, and access
D) Input, communications, filing, and security

The correct answer is B:) Input, processing, storage, and output.

145) A kilobyte equals how many bytes?

A) 10000 bytes
B) 10240 bytes
C) 1000 bytes
D) 1024 bytes

The correct answer is D:) 1024 bytes.

146) The stages of SDLC are, in order:

   A) Planning, Defining, Designing, Building, Testing, Deployment.
   B) Testing, Planning, Defining, Designing, Building, Deployment.
   C) Planning, Defining, Designing, Building, Deployment, Testing.
   D) Planning, Designing, Building, Defining, Testing, Deployment.

The correct answer is A:) Planning, Defining, Designing, Building, Testing, Deployment. SDLC stands for Systems Development Life Cycle.

147) In the diagram from question 15, what kind of component is the element labeled "Weekly Payroll System"?

   A) Process
   B) Subsystem
   C) Entity
   D) Data flow

The correct answer is A:) Process.

148) What does SQL stand for?

   A) Standard query language
   B) Structured query language
   C) Secondary query language
   D) System query language

The correct answer is B:) Structured query language.

149) What is SQL used for?

   A) To communicate with a database
   B) To optimize resources
   C) To develop web applications
   D) To communicate with a gaming system

The correct answer is A:) To communicate with a database.

150) What is a processing structure called that holds data in something similar a 3D spreadsheet rather than in a relational database?

   A) OIS square
   B) DSS cube
   C) OLAP cube
   D) TPS square

The correct answer is C:) OLAP cube.

151) Which of the following is a method of classifying and organizing information to make it more useful?

   A) Data organization
   B) Unstructured data
   C) Data adaptation
   D) Data streamlining

The correct answer is A:) Data organization.

152) How are ERP and TPS related?

   A) They are both informational databases
   B) They optimize resources
   C) They both develop data queries
   D) They are both organizational information systems

The correct answer is D:) They are both organizational information systems.

153) How is joint application design (JAD) used to design and develop an application?

   A) Through a joint application
   B) Through prototyping
   C) Through collaboration in workshops with members
   D) Through object-oriented analysis

The correct answer is C:) Through collaboration in workshops with members.

154) What is the difference between Agile and JAD/RAD?

- A) Agile is a framework and JAD/RAD are techniques for software development.
- B) There is no difference.
- C) Agile breaks down software while JAD/RAD develops software.
- D) Agile is a technique and JAD/RAD are frameworks for software development.

The correct answer is A:) Agile is a framework and JAD/RAD are techniques for software development.

155) How does CASE improve the CBIS development process?

- A) It decreases development costs.
- B) It reduces development backlogs.
- C) It automates every process of development.
- D) All of the above.

The correct answer is D:) All of the above.

156) EDI is the most commonly-used technique for which e-commerce format?

- A) B2B
- B) C2C
- C) B2C
- D) C2B

The correct answer is A:) B2B.

157) RAM is called what type of short-term memory?

- A) Analogous
- B) Random
- C) Non-volatile
- D) Volatile

The correct answer is D:) Volatile. If the power is shut off, all memory stored in RAM will be lost, therefore making it volatile.

158) What class of computer was the first computer system?

   A) Workstation
   B) Minicomputer
   C) Server
   D) Mainframe

The correct answer is D:) Mainframe.

159) Which of the following is an open source internet system?

   A) HTML5
   B) Mozilla Firefox
   C) Java
   D) PHP

The correct answer is B:) Mozilla Firefox.

160) What is the main difference between a worm and a Trojan horse?

   A) A Trojan horse is a virus, while a worm is not.
   B) A Trojan horse can replicate, unlike a worm.
   C) A worm can spread without any human interaction, while a Trojan horse must be invited onto the computer.
   D) A worm can physically damage computer hardware, while a Trojan horse cannot.

The correct answer is C:) A worm can spread without any human interaction, while a Trojan horse must be invited onto the computer.

161) Which of the following replicates itself?

   A) Virus
   B) Trojan horse
   C) Bot
   D) Worm

The correct answer is A:) Virus.

# Test-Taking Strategies

Here are some test-taking strategies that are specific to this test and to other DSST tests in general:

- Keep your eyes on the time. Pay attention to how much time you have left.

- Read the entire question and read all the answers. Many questions are not as hard to answer as they may seem. Sometimes, a difficult sounding question really only is asking you how to read an accompanying chart. Chart and graph questions are on most DANTES/DSST tests and should be an easy free point.

- If you don't know the answer immediately, the new computer-based testing lets you mark questions and come back to them later if you have time.

- Read the wording carefully. Some words can give you hints to the right answer. There are no exceptions to an answer when there are words in the question such as always, all or none. If one of the answer choices includes most or some of the right answers, but not all, then that is not the answer. Here is an example:

    The primary colors include all of the following:

    A) Red, Yellow, Blue, Green

    B) Red, Green, Yellow

    C) Red, Orange, Yellow

    D) Red, Yellow, Blue

- Although item A includes all the right answers, it also includes an incorrect answer, making it incorrect. If you didn't read it carefully, were in a hurry, or didn't know the material well, you might fall for this.

- Make a guess on a question that you do not know the answer to. There is no penalty for an incorrect answer. Eliminate the answer choices that you know are incorrect. For example, this will let your guess be a 1 in 3 chance instead.

# Test Preparation

How much you need to study depends on your knowledge of a subject. If you are interested in literature, took it in school, or enjoy reading then your study and preparation for the literature or humanities test will not need to be as intensive as that of someone who is new to literature.

This book is much different than the regular DANTES study guides. This book actually teaches you the information that you need to know to pass the test. If you are particularly interested in an area, or feel that you want more information, do a quick search online. We've tried not to include too much depth in areas that are not as essential on the test. Everything in this book will be on the test. It is important to understand all major theories and concepts listed in the table of contents. It is also important to know any bolded words.

Don't worry if you do not understand or know a lot about the area With minimal study, you can complete and pass the test.

One of the fallacies of other test books is test questions. People assume that the content of the questions are similar to what will be on the test. That is not the case. They are only there to test your "test taking skills" so for those who know to read a question carefully, there is not much added value from taking a "fake" test.

To prepare for the test, make a series of goals. Allot a certain amount of time to review the information you have already studied and to learn additional material. Take notes as you study; it will help you learn the material.

Legal Note

All rights reserved. This Study Guide, Book and Flashcards are protected under US Copyright Law. No part of this book or study guide or flashcards may be reproduced, distributed or stored in a retrieval system, or transmitted in any form or by any means, electronic, mechanical, photocopying, recording, or otherwise, without the prior written permission of the publisher Breely Crush Publishing LLC.

FLASHCARDS

This section contains flashcards for you to use to further your understanding of the material and test yourself on important concepts, names or dates. Read the term or question then flip the page over to check the answer on the back. Keep in mind that this information may not be covered in the text of the study guide. Take your time to study the flashcards, you will need to know and understand these concepts to pass the test.

Hardware	Software
ALU	ROM
Input Device	Output Device
Bit	Byte

Any program the runs on the computer	Anything that makes up the computer like the monitor, etc.
Read only memory	Arithmetic Logic Unit
Anything that retrieves information from the hard disk like the printer or monitor	Mouse, keyboard
Eight consecutive binary digits	Each binary digit

ASCII	GIGO
A kilobyte is how many bytes?	Who invented the first programmable calculating machine in 1835?
What is a site map?	LAN
Asynchronous	WAN

Garbage in, garbage out	American Standard Code for Information Interchange
Charles Babbage	1024
Local Area Network	High level diagrams that show system hierarchy
Wide Area Network	Sending one bit after the other

RAD	PERT
TPS	EDI
Tuples	A tree
SQL	CCU

Program Evaluation and Review Technique	Rapid Action Development
Electronic data interchange	Transaction processing system
Data hierarchy	Rows of a relation
Communication control units	Structured query language

Node	LAN style
SDLC	RAD
DSS	ESS
ES	KMS

| Ring or bus | Each computer in a network |

| Rapid application development | Traditional systems development life cycle |

| Executive support systems | Decision support systems |

| Knowledge management systems | Expert systems |

COBOL	MIS
CIS	CPU
Ergonomics	Assembler
Compiler	4GL

Management information systems	Common Business Oriented Language
Central processing unit	Computer information systems
Translates assembly language into machine code	The study of designing machines for more efficient and comfortable human use
Fourth generation languages	A program which translates an entire program into machine code, then executes the instructions

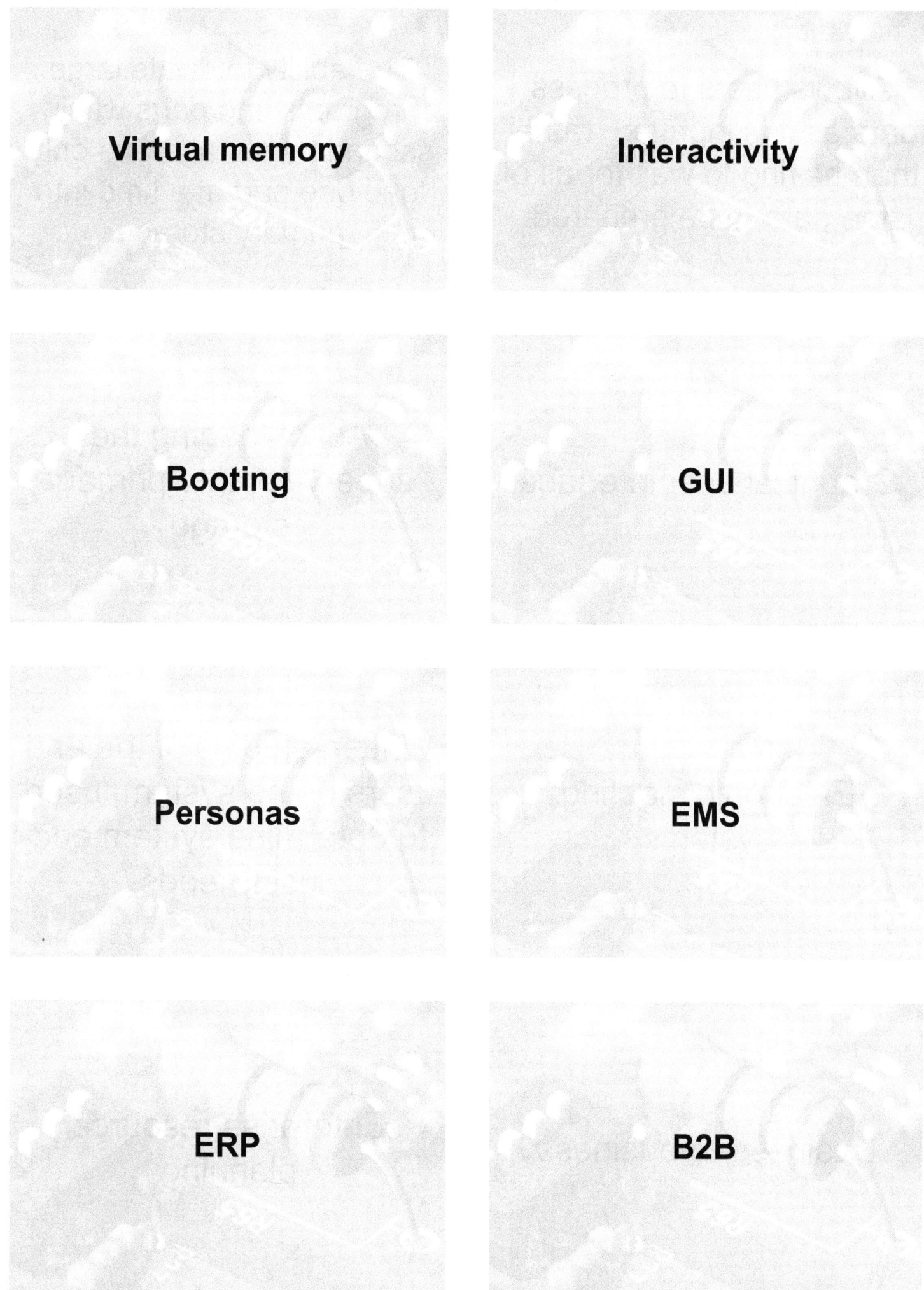

Allows users to process data as it is inputted, rather than having to wait for all of the data to be prepared	The ability to divide large programs into parts within secondary storage and only load one part at a time into primary storage
Graphical user interface	Act of loading the supervisor into primary storage
Electronic meeting systems	Written studies of the end users of the system, used to determine system and user needs
Business-to-business	Enterprise resource planning

www.ingramcontent.com/pod-product-compliance
Lightning Source LLC
Chambersburg PA
CBHW081830300426
44116CB00014B/2533